Teacher Recruitment and Retention
with a special focus on minority teachers

Antoine M. Garibaldi, Editor

Reference & Resource Series

nea PROFESSIONAL LIBRARY
National Education Association
Washington, D.C.

Copyright © 1989
National Education Association of the United States

Printing History
 First Printing: September 1989

Note

The opinions expressed in this publication should not be construed as representi
or position of the National Education Association. Materials published by the
sional Library are intended to be discussion documents for educators who are co
specialized interests of the profession.

Library of Congress Cataloging-in-Publication Data
Teacher recruitment and retention with a special focus on minority
teachers/Antoine M. Garaibaldi, editor.
  p.   cm. — (Reference & resource series)
 Bibliography: p.
 ISBN 0-8106-1538-X
  1. Teachers—United States—Selection and appointment. 2. Teacher
turnover—United States. 3. Minorities—Employment—United States.
I. Garibaldi, Antoine M. II. Series: Reference and resource series.
LB2835.25.T43   1989
371.1'0068'3—dc20   89-35851
                                    CIP

CONTENTS

Introduction, by Antoine M. Garibaldi 5

PART ONE—GLOBAL ISSUES OF MINORITY TEACHER RECRUITMENT

1. Recruitment: The Good News and the Bad News on the Teaching Profession,
   by Mary E. Dilworth 8

2. The Impact of School and College Reforms on the Recruitment of More Minority Teachers,
   by Antoine M. Garibaldi 11

3. State Action to Increase the Supply of Minority Teachers,
   by Denise Alston, Nathaniel Jackson, and Harvey Pressman 18

4. Recruiting and Retaining Minority Teachers: What Teacher Educators Can Do,
   by Jody Daughtry 25

PART TWO—INSTITUTIONAL RESPONSES

5. Minority Teacher Recruitment and Retention: A Potential Solution to a National Problem,
   by Gay C. Neuberger, Evangie H. McGlon, and Wanda M. Johnson 29

6. Increasing the Pool of Black Teachers: Plans and Strategies (Norfolk State University),
   by Elaine P. Witty 39

7. The Recruitment, Incentive, and Retention Programs for Minority Preservice Teachers (Georgia Southern College),
   by Livingston Alexander and John W. Miller 45

8. A Model Minority Teacher Recruitment and Retention Program: The Minority Teacher Preparation Program (MTP) (University of Wisconsin–Whitewater),
   by Bennett F. Berhow and Debra Knowles 51

9. New Challenges for Teacher Preparation Institutions: Recruitment and Retention (Auburn University),
   by Julia L. Willard and Bruce G. Gordon 56

PART THREE—RETENTION

10. Effective In-Service Techniques for Promoting Teacher Retention,
    by Ann Richardson Gayles 61

11. Developing Thoughtful Practitioners: A School/University Collaboration
for Retaining First-Year Teachers,
by Mary Gendernalik Cooper and Ann I. Morey 69

Appendixes 76
   A. Overview of Ethnic Minority Groups
      from NEA's ...*And Justice for All* 76
   B. Who Will Teach Minority Youth? 77

The Contributors 79

INTRODUCTION

One of the toughest jobs today in central office administration in school districts all across this country has to be that of the personnel director. Under this individual's leadership, forecasts for future human resources needs must be made in light of increasing elementary and secondary school enrollments, a smaller pool of teacher education graduates from which to choose, and a more seasoned and veteran group of teachers. The director and his/her recruiters, therefore, must develop strategic plans for personnel and be in a position to compete with other districts that are trying to attract the same group of prospective personnel. Their task is compounded even more by their need to hire more minority teachers, especially as the nonwhite school population grows, to replace those teachers who are leaving by retirement, those who are leaving to pursue other careers, and those who are leaving because of poor working conditions. The recruitment of new personnel is a major challenge for school districts but equally important is their ability to retain those teachers who are already teaching in the system. Because of the gravity and importance of the issue, teacher recruitment and retention demand realistic, creative, and innovative solutions. This book, therefore, is an attempt to address these issues from a variety of vantage points.

Even though there are some who doubt the magnitude of the future teaching shortage, one does not have to be a savant to recognize that there will be a need to replace American schools' current teaching force. As the most recent (1986) five-year survey of the American public school teacher by the National Education Association has indicated, the median age of teachers today is 41 (compared to 37 in 1981 and 33 in 1976); 69 percent are female and 31 percent are male; and almost 90 percent are white, 6.9 percent are Black, and the remaining 3 percent come from other nonwhite backgrounds (3).* Half of all teachers surveyed also had 15 or more years of experience and almost 28 percent had taught for more than 20 years in 1986 (compared to 14% in 1976). Taken one step further, more than one-third (35.6%) of all male teachers and close to one-fourth (23.8%) of all female teachers had 20 or more years of experience. The rate of entry of new teachers within the last five years has also been dropping dramatically. Where more than 35 percent of teachers surveyed by the NEA during the intervals between 1961 and 1976 had entered the profession within the previous five years, only 17 percent in 1981 and 10 percent in 1986 had been teaching for five years or less! The signs of an impending teacher shortage are very clear and our worries are not mollified by the fact that 46 percent of the teachers in the 1985-86 survey said that they planned to teach "until they were eligible to retire," compared to only 12 percent who said they would teach "until they were required to retire."

The obvious solution to this major problem is to prepare and train others to teach, but this is not easy as youth from all racial groups have more career choices than ever before. Young people today are more conscious of salaries, of promotional opportunities within professions, and also of the desire to live and work in comfortable surroundings. The overall declines in teacher education graduation rates have been well-documented over the last ten years by a variety of governmental agencies and researchers. However, even though there have been gradual percentage increases in the reported interest to teach by college freshmen in recent years, the actual numbers are still very low.

The picture for prospective teachers who are American Indian/Alaska Native, Asian and Pacific Islander, Black, and Hispanic is even more bleak. A 1988 enrollment survey, for example, conducted by the American Association of Colleges for Teacher Education that was specifically designed to assess the racial and ethnic representation of teacher education students states that "things are *worse* than the most informed educators have envisioned" (1). Their

---

*Numbers in parentheses appearing in the text refer to the References and/or Notes at the end of the chapter.

findings showed that a typical college of education with approximately 400 students included about 22 Black, 7 Hispanic, 3 Asian, and 2 American Indian/Alaska Native students. The AACTE report also indicated that the historically Black colleges, which represented 4 percent of the survey respondent group, enrolled more than 30 percent of the total group of Blacks in their undergraduate teacher education programs. [In many southern states, where the majority of historically Black colleges are located, these institutions' share of the states' Black teacher education graduates greatly exceed 50 percent, as this author and others have verified (2)].

Given the fact that minority enrollment in elementary and secondary schools increased in 44 states, and remained stable in four others between 1984 and 1986, it is important that more minority students be recruited to the teaching profession (4). This call for action is made more imperative by the fact that the proportion of nonwhite, especially Black, teachers has been declining. This need is very apparent among teachers and teacher educators and it is obvious as evidenced by the fact that the majority of manuscripts submitted to the NEA for this book focused on the recruitment and retention of minority teachers.

The book is divided into three sections: (1) global issues related to the teacher shortage; (2) institutional responses to the teacher shortage; and (3) retention of current school personnel.

In the first section, Dilworth begins by attempting to calm the cautious optimism that exists in teacher education, particularly as a result of recent enrollment gains and school/college collaborations. She emphasizes the great imbalance that exists between multicultural school populations and racially homogeneous teaching staffs. She not only counters some of the myths associated with the teaching shortage but also offers reasons and solutions for rapidly turning this situation around. Garibaldi's chapter follows with specific solutions and suggested reforms to increase the pool of more minority teachers by improving the academic achievement of nonwhite students in the early years so that they will be better prepared to enter college. In addition to addressing the "pipeline problem," he elaborates on how some teacher education reforms may diminish the number of prospective nonwhite teachers and suggests ways for making teaching careers more enticing to today's youth.

In the third chapter by Alston, Jackson, and Pressman, the authors present a variety of initiatives that have been implemented by states to increase the number of minority teachers. Through a collaborative project involving the Southern Education Foundation and the National Governors' Association, a regional task force of five states was established in 1987 to discuss initiatives already begun and to plan and develop activities and projects to abate the shortage of minority teachers within the participating states. And in the final chapter by Daughtry, the minority recruitment issue is addressed "from the inside" as teachers, teacher educators and college faculty are urged to assure that these students are not only admitted to education programs but that they graduate, are hired, and are retained by school districts.

The second section of the book provides several examples of what postsecondary institutions are already doing to increase the production of more minority teachers. In the initial chapter, Neuberger, McGlon, and Johnson present a very detailed and comprehensive proposal to attract students at the junior high and college levels, as well as from the ranks of teacher aides and nontraditional students. Funding, staffing, curricula, academic monitoring, and collaborative relationships are discussed. In the subsequent chapters, the authors discuss specific incentives and strategies that they have employed at their institutions: Witty at Norfolk State; Alexander and Miller at Georgia Southern; Berhow and Knowles at the University of Wisconsin-Whitewater; and Willard and Gordon at Auburn University-Montgomery. Each program varies and the discussions give readers program ideas that may be easily adaptable at their college or university.

The final two chapters of the last section are devoted to the retention of school personnel. In the first, Gayles promotes the use of orientations for new teachers, a variety of professional development activities as well as faculty involvement in school decision making to maintain the morale of teachers. The chapter effectively expresses the point of view that teachers must have supportive environments to work and grow in their profession. The last chapter by Cooper and Morey discusses an exciting collaborative project between San Diego State University and the San Diego Unified School District. The program is designed to give psychological, collegial, and instructional support to new teachers through organized seminars, release-day workshops, and classroom visits by university and school district personnel. There are several innovative features in this program but especially noteworthy is the involvement of faculty from arts and sciences disciplines, as well as the College of Education, and also broad representation from the school district staff. This type of support network is essential to first-year teachers' morale and confidence and it gives them the opportunity to improve their curricular skills as they begin their new careers. Retention strategies, therefore, are just as important to stabilizing a teaching force that will undoubtedly become younger as veteran educators retire and pursue other midcareer opportunities.

—Antoine M. Garibaldi

REFERENCES

1. American Association of Colleges for Teacher Education. *Teacher Education Pipeline: Schools, Colleges and Departments of Education Enrollments by Race and Ethnicity.* Washington, DC: AACTE, 1988.

2. Garibaldi, Antoine M. *The Decline of Teacher Production in Louisiana (1976–1983) and Attitudes Toward the Profession.* Atlanta: Southern Education Foundation, March 1986; Trent, William. "Equity Consideration in Higher Education: Race and Sex Differences in Degree Attainment and Major Fields from 1976 through 1981." *American Journal of Education* (May 1984).

3. National Education Association. *Status of the American Public School Teacher 1985-86.* Washington, DC: the Association, July 1987.

4. U.S. Department of Education, Office for Civil Rights. "1984 and 1986 Elementary and Secondary Civil Rights Survey." Washington, DC: U.S. Department of Education, Office for Civil Rights, October 1986 and December 1987.

1. RECRUITMENT: THE GOOD NEWS AND THE BAD NEWS ON THE TEACHING PROFESSION

by Mary E. Dilworth

The recent call for more quality teachers to staff the nation's classrooms has not gone unheeded. Colleges for teacher education have enjoyed a 20 percent increase in enrollment over the past four years, and today's education students are as bright as their peers who are pursuing other occupations (1). The literature is ripe with information regarding the "knowledge base" necessary for good teaching, and there is much discussion and activity on relating research to practice. Kindergarten (K)-12 and school, college, and Department of Education (SCDE) collaboration projects are proliferating, and intern/mentor teaching programs offer new teachers an easier transition from college to the classroom than has previously been available. The school restructuring movement promises greater acknowledgment of teachers' professional abilities, and salaries that will compensate their efforts in a greater way than in the past.

Much good surrounds teaching and teacher education today, and if it were not for the notable absence of racial and ethnic diversity within teachings' ranks, a celebration might be in order. The nation's teaching force is aging rapidly and in the process, the profession's minority representation is diminishing. The majority of students who are pursuing a teaching career today are neither racial/ethnic minorities nor are they from areas predominated by minorities.

Thirty-three states have K-12 minority enrollments of 20 percent or more; however, only six states have SCDE enrollments greater than 15 percent. Nearly 95 percent of education students are from rural and suburban areas and intend to return to those areas on completion of their studies. Few potential teachers welcome a teaching assignment in the inner city or working with students with limited English proficiency. The college faculty who teach education students are, by and large white, and, for the most part, have not had extensive experiences in urban city schools (1).

In essence, there are few in the teacher education pipeline that are or will be able to inherently understand or communicate the educational needs of minority youth, and engineer their educational achievement. Try as we might, it is virtually impossible to truly educate a multicultural population with a homogeneous teaching force.

By now almost everyone has heard or witnessed the fact that we are fast becoming a nation predominated by people of color. In the next century, the "minority" presence will be undeniable in virtually every region of the country. In preparation for this certainty, the nation has done a fine job of defining equity, justice, and multiculturalism, terms that are crucial to a functional co-existence of various racial/ethnic groups. Unfortunately, the nation has done a poor job of translating these concepts into educational achievement.

The shortage of minority teachers has been on the periphery of the educational reform discussion and movement, and as a consequence, has not garnered the level of activity and resources necessary to effectively recruit significant numbers of Black, Hispanic, Asian-American, and American Indian students into teaching. For the most part, existing programs are operating in isolation and do not reflect concerted efforts on the part of government, schools, colleges, and the community. The gains in the numbers of minorities entering the teaching profession have been very small, and it is clear that without a unified effort, very little will be accomplished.

There are a number of areas that need attention in order to achieve consensus of thought and significant action on this issue. They are areas relevant to all groups, i.e., educators, policymakers, and the community at large. They entail three basic activities: attitudinal changes, dissemination of information, and monitoring.

Changing attitudes may be a difficult task but it can be accomplished by dispelling untruths. For instance, it is a commonly held belief that the reason that there are not enough minorities going into teaching is that students are now choosing other occupations that were not previously open to them. The truth is that students are going into new and more popular fields; however, a smaller percentage of minority students are entering college today than they were ten years ago (4). There are also more minority students in the nation today than there were ten years ago and not as many as there will be tomorrow. Academic and financial support programs must be established that will encourage and assist a greater number of minority students to enter and complete college at the baccalaureate level. Schools of engineering, business, and education may be brimming over with students, but not with minority students.

Another myth that must be dispelled is that high performance on teacher certification examinations indicates that an individual will be good and effective in the classroom. A sound knowledge base is crucial to good teaching; however, the ability to transmit that knowledge is of equal importance and is not something that is being effectively gauged by the tests in use today. It is important for everyone to understand that not all minorities perform poorly on tests and that all minority students do not have the same deficiencies. Unless this particular myth is dispelled, every minority teacher, by implication, will be perceived as less effective and not as bright as others.

Poor compensation for teachers has been identified as a deterrent to increasing the number of minority teachers. While teacher salaries have been going up, they are not as high as those of doctors, lawyers, or engineers, and likely never will be. We need far more teachers than we do doctors and lawyers. Basic economics suggest that we can do a better job in compensating teachers but cannot afford to pay all teachers at rates comparable to the "prestige" professions. If we consider for a moment the large number of children "at risk," children of children who have been on welfare their entire life (and who will likely continue to be unless something is done), it seems apparent that for these students a starting salary of approximately $18,000 a year is a good beginning. For those students apt to enter what sociologists term the "permanent underclass," a good teaching job may be salvation.

The good news about teaching must be shared with the community at large. The public must learn to show greater respect for and learn to acknowledge the contributions that a good teacher brings to the quality of life. All parents should recognize and acknowledge effective minority teachers instead of shying away from them, as they sometimes do, when given a choice.

Recognition of good teachers in the community should be an ongoing event. This helps to raise the image of the teacher as a professional and shows students a very positive side of a noble and worthwhile profession. Students can become more acquainted with the practical aspects of teaching early on. They can be employed to assist with younger children in day-care programs, after school, and in the summers. In this manner, they can learn information from the teacher and gain skills that will be useful to them if they should choose to become teachers. Certainly, these skills will be useful when they eventually become parents.

New teachers to a school system, of any color, should be offered an orientation to the community and to the neighborhood. Community organizations and churches, for example, are excellent resources for this type of activity. For the next decade at least, there will be a large number of white teachers in schools composed primarily of Black and Hispanic youngsters. Unfortunately, these teachers often do not get all the training that they need either to understand or to be especially effective with children of color.

Generally speaking, national organizations, state and federal officials have a firm grasp on the national education picture and trends but it is difficult for them to identify areas of greatest need unless people in those areas inform them.

For instance, national data indicate that the state of Mississippi's K–12 public school minority population is well over 50 percent (mostly Black). Approximately 22 percent of the students in teacher education are Black, but it is a state and local responsibility to identify school districts where this situation is exemplified, i.e., where there are significant numbers of Black students, and few, if any, Black teachers. Local education administrators, teachers, and parents must look for areas of shortage—in schools and in districts—and share this information with state and local officials. Enough real-life incidents may prompt action for a remedy.

Local school systems and institutions must be monitored. Are minority students being encouraged or discouraged into entering four-year colleges? Are they taking the courses that will qualify them for entry? Are the colleges in the community recruiting athletes from the urban centers and students from the suburbs?

We cannot assume that a school board knows that three Black teachers are retiring from a particular school in a given year. We cannot assume that the school system personnel office knows that the community wants these vacancies to be filled with Black teachers. We cannot assume that the personnel office knows or is willing to actively recruit teachers from historically Black institutions rather than competing, possibly unsuccessfully, for the very few minority teacher education graduates from the local predominantly white institution.

Lastly, and most importantly, we must review legislation and state policies before they are enacted. If 10 state scholarships are proposed for minority students entering science—the door is already open. It is probable that the legislature can also find money for at least five education students who will eventually teach the future scientists, doctors, and lawyers of America.

Given the number of intelligent and talented Black, Hispanic, American Indian, and Asian-American students in the nation's schools, the current shortage of minority teachers is inexcusable. It is incumbent upon educators, policymakers, and the community at large to develop broad-based, appropriate, and effective strategies to correct the problem.

SELECTED REFERENCES

Note: The majority of this text is drawn from a paper prepared for the NAACP Annual Convention, July 11, 1988.

1. American Association of Colleges for Teacher Education. *Teaching Teachers Facts and Figures: 1987.* Washington, DC: AACTE, 1988.

2. _____. *Teaching Teachers Facts and Figures: 1988.* Washington, DC: AACTE, 1989.

3. _____. *Teacher Education Pipeline: SCDE Enrollments by Race and Ethnicity.* Washington, DC: AACTE, 1989.

4. American Council on Education. *Minority Enrollment in Higher Education, 1987.* Washington, DC: ACE, 1988.

2. THE IMPACT OF SCHOOL AND COLLEGE REFORMS ON THE RECRUITMENT OF MORE MINORITY TEACHERS

by Antoine M. Garibaldi

The success of the education reforms promulgated during the early 1980s rests largely on Amerca's ability to maintain an adequate, highly able, and diverse teaching force. But only recently has the teacher supply issue obtained the kind of attention it so critically deserves. Although its importance has sometimes been lost in the numerous recommendations for restructuring the preservice training of teachers, it has become more and more evident that shortages are imminent as the current teaching force, which has a median age of approximately 41 and a mean of 16 years of teaching experience in 1987, grows older and continues to retire earlier (1). Additionally, the likelihood of this teaching shortage occurring sooner than expected has been hastened by the significant national decline in the number of teacher education graduates since the early 1970s.

This teacher supply issue has tremendous significance in major metropolitan school districts where almost half of the school population is already nonwhite. Because estimates suggest that at least one-third of all school children will be nonwhite by the year 2000, and more than 53 major metropolitan school districts will have majority nonwhite enrollments by the turn of the century, there is increasing concern over the rapid decline of minority teachers (2). This chapter is devoted chiefly to the latter issue, with special emphasis focused on the development and expansion of the pool of nonwhite teachers.

While much consideration has been given more recently to the improved preparation of future teachers through the plans of the Holmes Group and the Carnegie Task Force on Teaching as a Profession, insufficient emphasis has been placed on the recruitment of more nonwhite teachers. Both groups have advocated the need for stronger liberal arts preparation, differentiated and higher salaries, and more rigorous admissions requirements for prospective teachers. This author supports the goals of these groups but believes that a more salient issue to be addressed is whether these sweeping reforms will increase the pool of teachers, and especially nonwhite teachers, to maintain the ethnic and racial diversity that has become a hallmark of America's educational system.

Recent articles by this author and others have documented the dwindling supply of Black teachers since they account for the major share, almost 80 percent, of nonwhite teachers in the classroom today (3). Compared to 1979 when nonwhite teachers represented 11.1 percent of the teaching force, in 1987 they accounted for 10.3 percent. More specifically, Blacks represent 6.9 percent today compared to 8.6 percent in 1979; Hispanics 1.9 percent versus 1.8 percent; Asian and Pacific Islanders 0.9 percent compared to 0.5 percent; and American Indians/Alaska Natives 0.6 percent versus 0.2 percent in 1979 (4). These data indicate that today's pupils as well as the next generation's youth will see fewer role models in the classroom unless something is done immediately to confront this problem.

This chapter is primarily concerned with the identification and implementation of critical reforms that should increase the pool of prospective nonwhite teachers. Specifically it argues that:

1. Preparation of minority students in elementary and secondary schools must be improved to assure a larger pool of prospective education majors.

2. More attention should be devoted to increasing the retention and graduation rates of minority students in all postsecondary institutions.

3. The impact of current standardized testing on nonwhite students may exacerbate the shortage of minority teachers; and, teacher licensing examinations should be redesigned and incorporate the theoretical knowledge of the teaching profession.

4. Specific teacher reforms may weaken the role of historically Black colleges in the preparation of more nonwhite teachers for the next century.

5. Teaching must be both financially and professionally attractive to minority students (i.e., competitive salaries, professional advancement, scholarships for extended preservice teacher training programs in college, etc.).

Each of these topics is discussed separately in the subsequent sections.

IMPROVING ELEMENTARY AND SECONDARY SCHOOLING

In any discussion on the decline and shortage of nonwhite teachers in America, common reasons always surface. The list typically includes: increased certification requirements in many states; poor performance by nonwhite students on the National Teachers Examination and other certification and competency tests; low salaries and limited promotional opportunities in teaching; more career opportunities for minorities in other fields and their observed shift toward other majors in college; substandard working conditions in many schools; and the negative attention that education has received in the media. All are indeed plausible reasons for the existing decline and each explanation has had some impact on both the number and types of students—white and nonwhite—who have chosen *not* to major in education. But this author and others, notably Patricia A. Graham, have argued that significant academic improvements must take place first in our elementary and secondary schools to assure that there will be a large enough pool from which to draw a talented cadre of nonwhite students who can be effective teachers (5).

In more simplistic and practical terms, the educational pipeline needs a major overhaul to guarantee minorities equal and competitive career, as well as advanced educational, opportunities. Too many young children are entering school without the necessary readiness skills, thus minimizing their academic success as well as progression in the early grades. Because of unsatisfactory performance on standardized tests in the basic skills, many at the next educational level prematurely lose interest in learning and still more are dropping out during the junior high school years. For those who reach ninth grade, the prospect of their finishing high school is bleak and it is not uncommon to find school systems where more than 40 percent of their ninth-graders do not reach twelfth grade.

While some will finish their education by obtaining a General Equivalency Diploma, colleges and universities are already experiencing decreased enrollments of nonwhites in their institutions. But unfortunately, the declines have come when the pool of 18- to 24-year-old nonwhites, especially Blacks and Hispanics, has increased. More early childhood education is needed for these youth, and curricula at elementary and secondary levels must be redesigned to assure that these pupils know how to think and apply what they have learned to postsecondary or vocational situations. If more nonwhite students are academically prepared to enter college, then the pool of potential minority education majors is automatically increased.

INCREASING RETENTION AND GRADUATION RATES IN COLLEGE

At the postsecondary level, fewer nonwhite students are attending, matriculating, and graduating from college. For Blacks, the number and proportion of students enrolled in college should be much higher, given their current population demographics. For example, between 1976 and 1986, the percentage of Black students who graduated from high school increased from 67.5 percent to 76.4 percent; but the participation rate of Black high school graduates who were enrolled in college ranged from a high of 33.4 percent in 1976 to a low of 26.1 percent in 1985 (6).

In 1986, Blacks represented only 8.6 percent of the college population, compared to 9.6 percent in 1976. Though this percentage decline appears to be small, it represents a 10 percent decline of Black students in college and a static enrollment of slightly more than one million Black students over this ten-year period. Moreover, given the larger size of the age cohort and the larger numbers of Blacks graduating from high school between 1976 and 1986, Black enrollment should have increased by at least 20 percent, had it been possible to capitalize on those gains. Equally important to this discussion is the fact that 43 percent of all Black students in college are enrolled at two-year institutions, but barely 15 percent transfer to four-year institutions (7). However, as will be seen later, completion of a baccalaureate degree must take precedence over enrollment and admissions statistics to increase the cadre of Black teachers.

The analysis for other racial groups attending college shows some positive percentage gains in enrollment but the proportion of high school graduates between 1976 and 1986 who actually attended is still down. The percentage of Hispanic students in college in 1986 was 5 percent, compared to a share of 3.5 percent in 1976. Asian and Pacific Islanders represented 3.6 percent of college enrollment in 1986, compared to 1.8 percent in 1976; and the percentage of American Indian/Alaska Native students in college during that ten-year period was the same (0.7 percent) (8). However, like Blacks, Hispanics' proportion of high school graduates who went to college between 1976 and 1986 declined from 33.4 to 28.6 percent at a time when their enrollment should have risen dramatically in absolute numbers because of a 62 percent increase in the size of their 18- to 24-year-old cohort (9). Finally, almost half (47%) of all minority students, especially Hispanic, American Indian/Alaska Native, and Black students, are disproportionally enrolled in two-year colleges in 1986, compared to 37 percent of white students in college (10).

As stated earlier, college degree attainment for nonwhite students is even more important than their mere participation in postsecondary education. Comparisons of graduation data always indicate that only white students receive proportionally more bachelor's degrees than their enrollment percentages within higher education. For example, whites accounted for 80.2 percent of undergraduate enrollments in 1984 and they accounted for 88.3 percent of the baccalaureate degree recipients in the 1984-85 academic year. Asian and Pacific Islanders constituted 3.2 percent but received 2.9 percent of the degrees. Hispanics and American Indian/Alaska Natives represented 4.4 and 0.7 percent of total enrollment in 1984, but received only 2.9 and 0.6 percent of the degrees in 1984-85, respectively. For Blacks, who represented 8.8 percent of total enrollment in 1984, their share of all bachelor's degrees was only 6.2 percent (11).

The foregoing discussion underscores what this author believes is the second critical step for halting the rapid shortage of nonwhite teachers in America. Stated more bluntly, institutions of higher education, especially two-year and four-year colleges and universities, must carefully monitor the academic performance of all minority students and provide effective support systems to facilitate their successful matriculation, retention, and eventual graduation. Regardless of the majors minority students choose when entering college, all should be considered as prospective teacher education candidates either after graduation (e.g., in secondary fields) or during college (e.g., students who have undeclared majors, those who change their majors, or those students who may elect to minor in education because they have some interest in teaching as an alternative career choice). Therefore, as this broader view of an expanded pool of potential education majors is taken, more importance must be given to increasing the retention and graduation rates of all minority students in colleges and universities.

THE IMPACT OF STANDARDIZED TESTING ON MINORITY TEACHERS

Another major influence that will affect the size of the minority teaching pool is student performance on assessment measures. Minimum SAT or ACT college entrance scores that are now required in some states for education majors will undoubtedly shrink the pool of talented nonwhite students even further. Some states already require minimum ACT scores ranging between 16 and 18 for prospective education majors. However, 1988 data indicate that Blacks' ACT mean was 13.6 compared to whites' average of 19.6 and a national mean of 18.8. Thus, many nonwhite students who may have had good academic records in high school but who may not have performed well on college entrance tests are automatically excluded from majoring in education. Similar exclusionary policies that require successful performance by education majors on a sophomore level competency test have already had deleterious effects in some states.

G. Pritchy Smith's recent state-by-state study for the National Education Association and the Council of Chief State School Officers on the effects of competency testing on the supply of minority teachers has documented the current impact of the above policies. Smith states:

> The testing requirements, including minimum SAT and ACT scores, for entry into teacher education restrict so severely the pool of minority candidates in most states that special recruiting programs and loan and scholarship incentive programs are rendered ineffective in increasing the number of minority teachers. In one state with a public school minority enrollment of 32 percent and with a graduating high school class of 3,761 Black test-takers and 2,918 Hispanic test-takers, 80 percent of the Blacks and 61 percent of the Hispanics failed to post SAT scores high enough to be admitted to teacher education programs. (12)

With respect to teacher competency and certification tests, Smith provides evidence that these tests also screen out large numbers of prospective nonwhite teachers at the completion of a teacher education program. His data show that "the elimination of approximately 32,933 minority candidates and teachers, including 19,499 Blacks, 8,172 Hispanics, 1,562 Asians, 687 Native Americans, and 3,013 other minorities can be documented in nineteen states." Low passing rates of minorities on competency tests before their junior year of study, on teacher certification exams at the end of their preservice training in college, and more recently, competency testing of veteran teachers have had compounding effects on both the current supply and recruitment of prospective nonwhite teachers. In addition to screening out young people who are interested in a career in teaching, these assessment measures and criteria also discourage others who may be inclined toward the field but apprehensive about the tests.

This author recognizes that tests to obtain teacher certification are not likely to be eliminated and believes that lowering minimum qualifying scores will not substantially increase the numbers and quality of minority teachers. But there is agreement with Linda Darling-Hammond that teacher certification tests must better reflect the professional knowledge base of educational and psychological theory, research, and facts related to teaching and learning, rather than the simple recognition of facts within subject areas, knowledge of school law and bureaucracy, and the identification of situation-specific teaching behaviors in hypothetical teaching scenarios. As Darling-Hammond has concluded from analyses of current teacher tests, these instruments "do not allow for demonstrations of teacher knowledge, judgment and skill in the kinds of complex settings that characterize real teaching" (13). Thus, unless more attention is devoted to instructional content on these tests, she believes that the measures will neither serve the purpose of professionalizing teaching nor assess the fundamental knowledge that teachers should have.

THE IMPACT OF TEACHER REFORMS ON BLACK COLLEGES

Any optimistic speculation on the future of minorities in teaching should always include the historically Black colleges as a major producer of nonwhite teachers for the next century. For many years the preparation of teachers has been a primary mission of these institutions, but some have had to reconsider this role as Black students have chosen to major in more popular fields such as business, public affairs and services, the allied health professions, and other scientific fields. Recent state policies governing teacher education programs, especially in the South where most of these institutions are located, as well as the anticipated reforms of the Carnegie and Holmes groups have also caused some to ponder how education programs will fare at these colleges and universities. Nevertheless, the best hope for maintaining the numbers of Black teachers depends on these institutions because of their past and continued record of producing Black teachers for the nation's schools.

While data have indicated that historically Black colleges graduated almost half (48%) of all Black undergraduates in education in this country in 1981, there has been a significant national decline in the absolute number of nonwhite education majors and degree recipients (14). The same negative trend in education enrollment has been true also for white students but the potential obstacles for increasing the number and percentage of nonwhite teachers at historically Black colleges are more acute.

The institutional impact of the current reform movement on historically Black colleges could significantly decrease the future supply of minority teachers. Historically and predominantly Black colleges and universities, as well as other institutions that have traditionally dedicated their mission to preparing large numbers of nonwhite teachers, may not have sufficient financial resources to add faculty or to restructure their teacher education programs, as proposed by the Carnegie and Holmes groups, because of their already low enrollments. Not only will competition for these students become more fierce with other institutions who can offer more financial incentives, but there is also the likelihood that some teacher education programs at those schools may be abolished because of state policies that require a predetermined percentage of their graduates to pass certification tests. In Florida, for example, at least 80 percent of teacher education graduates at each institution must pass the state competency examination in order for the college or university to maintain state teacher accreditation approval. Similar policies have been adopted in other states and these legislative requirements will have a major impact on education enrollments where nonwhite students have been traditionally prepared for teaching careers. These and other similar policies can have potentially adverse "second generation" effects on the Black colleges' role of preparing a critical mass of nonwhite teachers (15).

MAKING TEACHING FINANCIALLY AND PROFESSIONALLY ATTRACTIVE

Finally, the effective recruitment of academically talented nonwhite youth to the teaching field will also require significant financial incentives to be competitive with other disciplines and career options. Colleges and universities, as well as state and federal governments, will need to provide more scholarships, grants and forgivable loans, especially if an extra year of training is added to preservice education programs. Moreover, teacher salaries must be increased nationally and especially in major metropolitan school districts.

It is also important for teaching to be recognized as a profession where there are opportunities for advancement. Some states and school districts have already implemented programs not only to reward effective teaching but also to keep outstanding teachers in the classroom. Thus, as prospective teachers see positive signs of professional advancement opportunities in the field, they may be more inclined to choose teaching as a career.

CONCLUSION

In addition to the preceding concerns, several barriers will have to be overcome if there is to be a representative number and percentage of minority teachers by the turn of the century. First, the impact of assessment measures that serve as prerequisite entrance criteria for admission to college and teacher education programs and that screen out large numbers of nonwhite students should be seriously studied. In many instances, using the test as a sole criterion penalizes students who may not be good test-takers but who may have good academic records.

Second, state policies that are targeted at the elimination of institutions' teacher education programs, if sufficient percentages of students do not achieve qualifying scores on certification exams, should be more sensitive to the larger impact on colleges and universities and also on student enrollments. Even though such policies have been established to improve the quality of teacher education graduates, these statutes in most instances fail to recognize the traditionally poor performance of nonwhite students on all types of standardized instruments. To penalize the institutions where large numbers of these students attend is tantamount to "throwing the baby out with the bath water."

Third, and related to the previous recommendation, major strategies and programs should be developed to help nonwhite students perform better on standardized tests throughout the education system. Several historically Black institutions have made great strides in improving the percentage of their students who pass certification and competency exams, but the percentages mask the severe decline of Black education graduates. And finally, recruitment of nonwhite students into teacher education programs must be initiated and nurtured at the junior and senior high school levels with the assistance of colleges and universities.

It is important to note here that a September 1987 policy statement of the American Association of Colleges for Teacher Education has endorsed specific strategies to increase minority teacher recruitment and retention. AACTE's recommendations comprehensively target support from federal, state and local agencies, as well as encourage the collaboration of high schools and postsecondary institutions. Some examples include national and state scholarship programs; targeted work-study programs for high school and college students who are planning to teach; collaborative projects between two-year and four-year colleges; as well as incentive programs whereby midcareer professionals can obtain a master's degree in teaching (16). Congressional action, however, will be needed to assure that these programs receive adequate financial support.

The future of minorities in teaching will depend on the ability of society, local communities, schools, the media, parents and others to convince young minority students of the importance of becoming teachers. Society, however, will have to provide the necessary financial aid for education majors and competitive salaries for teachers to assure that these youth view teaching as a rewarding career and one where they can be effective role models and academic trainers of the next generation. If meaningful and sensitive attention is devoted to these matters, the goal of maintaining an equitable and diverse supply of quality minority teachers can be achieved.

NOTES

1. See the Carnegie Foundation for the Advancement of Teaching, *The Condition of Teaching: A State-by-State Analysis, 1988* (Princeton, NJ: Princeton University Press, 1988); C. Emily Feistritzer, *The Condition of Teaching: A State-by-State Analysis* (Princeton, NJ: Carnegie Foundation for the Advancement of Teaching, 1985); and U.S. Department of Education (Center for Education Statistics), *The 1985 Public School Survey: Early Tabulations* (Washington, DC: U.S. Department of Education, November 1986).

2. Margaret E. Goertz and Barbara Pitcher, *The Impact of NTE Use by States on Teacher Selection* (Princeton, NJ: Educational Testing Service, 1985).

3. See Mary E. Dilworth, *Teachers' Totter* (Washington, DC: Institute for the Study of Educational Policy, Howard University, 1984); G. Pritchy Smith, "The Critical Issue of Excellence and Equity in Competency Testing," *Journal of Teacher Education* 35, no. 2 (1984); Joan C. Baratz, "Black Participation in the Teacher Pool" (Paper prepared for the Carnegie Task Force on Teaching as a Profession, 1984); Patricia A. Graham, "Black Teachers: A Drastically Scarce Resource," *Phi Delta Kappan* (April 1987); Antoine M. Garibaldi, "The Paradoxical Impact of Affirmative Action on the Supply of Black Teachers," *Journal of Educational Policy* 2, no. 2 (1988).

4. Data on 1979 rates are from the U.S. Department of Education's National Center for Education Statistics, *The Condition of Education, 1982* (Washington, DC: U.S. Government Printing Office, 1982) and 1987 data are from a report of the National Education Association, *Status of the American Public School Teacher, 1985–86* (Washington, DC: the Association, July 1987).

5. See Antoine M. Garibaldi, "Quality and Diversity in Schools: The Case for an Expanded Pool of Minority Teachers" (Paper prepared for the American Association of Colleges for Teacher Education's Wingspread Policy Forum, Washington, DC, August 1987); and Patricia A. Graham, "Black Teachers: A Drastically Scarce Resource."

6. Reginald Wilson and Deborah Carter, *Minorities in Higher Education* (Washington, DC: American Council on Education, November 1988).

7. College Board, *Equality and Excellence: The Educational Status of Black Americans* (New York: College Entrance Examination Board, 1985).

8. Center for Educational Statistics, "Trends in Minority Enrollment in Higher Education, Fall 1976–Fall 1986" (Washington, DC: U.S. Department of Education, Office of Educational Research and Improvement, April 1988).

9. Reginald Wilson and Deborah Carter, *Minorities in Higher Education*.

10. Center for Education Statistics, "Trends in Minority Enrollment in Higher Education, Fall 1976–Fall 1986."

11. Center for Educational Statistics, "Racial/Ethnic Data for 1984 Fall Enrollment and Earned Degree Recipi-

ents for Academic Year 1984–85'' (Washington, DC: U.S. Department of Education, Office of Educational Research and Improvement, January 1988).

12. G. Pritchy Smith, *The Effects of Competency Testing on the Supply of Minority Teachers* (Jacksonville, FL: University of North Florida, September 1987). This report was prepared as a joint product of the National Education Association and the Council of Chief State School Officers. The data were cited in Smith's September 1987 revision.

13. Linda Darling-Hammond, "Teaching Knowledge: How Do We Test It?" *American Educator* (Fall 1986).

14. William Trent, "Equity Considerations in Higher Education: Race and Sex Differences in Degree Attainment and Major Fields from 1976 through 1981,'' *American Journal of Education* (May 1984).

15. For more on these issues, see Antoine M. Garibaldi, "Recruitment, Admissions and Standards: Black Teachers and the Holmes and Carnegie Reports," *Metropolitan Education* (Spring 1987).

16. Specific details of these programs are described in the American Association of Colleges for Teacher Education policy statement, "Minority Teacher Recruitment and Retention: A Call for Action" (Washington, DC: AACTE, September 1987).

3. STATE ACTION TO INCREASE THE SUPPLY OF MINORITY TEACHERS

by Denise Alston, Nathaniel Jackson, and Harvey Pressman

INTRODUCTION

In the fall of 1987, the Southern Education Foundation (SEF) convened a five-state task force to address the problem of minority teacher shortages. Supported by matching funds from the National Governors' Association (NGA) and SEF, the Southern Regional Task Force on the Supply of Minority Teachers was organized to facilitate the work of five separate state task forces appointed by the governors to address the problem: What can our state do to increase the supply of minority teachers (especially Blacks), in both the immediate future and the long run?

The regional task force, made up of representatives from Arkansas, Georgia, North Carolina, Tennessee, and Virginia, met five times between November 1987, and May 1988. Delegates discussed alternate strategies by which states could increase public awareness of the need for more minority teachers and develop new practices that could slow the precipitous decline in their numbers. Each state task force developed a concrete plan to deal with this problem, and made specific recommendations to their respective governors. The background of these efforts, and the specific results follow.

IN-STATE ACTIVITIES

Over the past five years, individual states have begun to take the lead in demonstrating what can be done to deal with various aspects of the minority teacher shortage problem. In data collection and analysis, Illinois and Florida might show the way. In terms of planning for the future, Missouri and Maryland took some interesting early steps. With respect to "pipeline" strategies, Alabama and South Carolina initiated promising programs. In developing financial aid incentives, North Carolina and Florida have organized new approaches. In reinforcing support for the historically Black colleges and universities, which have traditionally produced the bulk of the Black teaching force in America, South Carolina and North Carolina have provided funding for interesting new initiatives. In terms of promoting strategies designed to have some immediate impact on the problem in the short term, Maryland and, again, South Carolina have devised innovative new steps. And all of these activities have served as a base on which the five task forces in the states involved in the SEF/NGA project have tried to build. Let's look at some examples.

Minority Teacher Development and Recruitment Activities

Information Gathering. The most important initial step a state can take is to study teacher supply and demand taking into account the race and ethnicity of the current and projected teaching force. Collecting reliable statewide data on minority teachers and teacher candidates was found to be the most difficult task encountered by the fifteen states. Several states did not collect or report teacher (or student) data by race.

A good example of data gathering is the Illinois State Board of Education and State Teacher Certification Board's report, "A Study of Teacher Trends and Traits." The report was required by the 1985 Illinois educational reform legislation, and presented a thorough analysis of the gender and minority distribution of students enrolled in colleges of education and teachers. These data were analyzed in the context of the past and current minority student enrollment. The data showed parts of the state where minority teachers were working, where minority students were enrolled, and the size of the pool of future minority teachers.

Florida's Education Standards Commission produced a similar report on meeting the challenge of providing minority teachers to their public schools. This 1987 report also included specific recommendations on how the state could increase the supply of minority teachers and improve data collection on ers. The recommendations include a statewide study on the causes of teacher attrition and the systematic follow-up of college of education graduates.

Planning. In South Carolina, in 1984, the deans of several colleges of education provided leadership for forming a task force to plan for a teacher recruitment center. The task force developed a proposal and submitted it to the Higher Education Commission, where it was turned into successful legislation that resulted in the formation of the South Carolina Center for Teacher Recruitment. The Center's initial annual budget was $250,000. The Center is a consortium of representatives from twenty-six teacher training institutes, public school educators, legislators, business people, and representatives from state education agencies and professional associations. Through the Center, the state intends to make a concerted effort to compete with business, industry, and the professions for talented people. The Center focuses its recruitment efforts on individuals of above-average academic ability who feel some inclination to teach, but may be discouraged by peers, parents, or teachers.

Illinois has begun its planning process with a different approach. Last year, the State Board of Education and State Higher Education Board created a joint committee of educators, business people, and community activists who will create recommendations for improving minority student achievement and recruiting and retaining minority teachers. They will consider existing research findings and presentations by institutional and program representatives in developing the recommendations.

The Missouri Department of Education has created an internal task force that is exploring ways to increase minority recruitment. The task force members represent teacher education, urban education, desegregation technical assistance, and the deputy commissioner of public instruction.

The state school superintendent in Maryland appointed a task force on minority teacher recruitment and promotion. The task force's charge is to submit an action plan to the superintendent that reflects its assessment of minority teacher recruitment strategies and local systems' promotion policies. The action plan may result in recommendations for programs and practices or requests to the legislature for funds. The report was released in spring 1988.

Strategies to Improve the Pipeline. Planning activities informed by the needs and resources of individual states can focus minority teacher recruitment efforts on a variety of target groups. Some states have begun by targeting young adolescents still in the middle grades to raise aspirations and to provide academic assistance. Other states provide students with early exposure to teaching experiences in order to recruit them into the profession. Still others have started by focusing on access to higher education by providing financial aid or other incentives. Some states have begun by building on the importance of historically Black colleges in preparing Black teachers and, thus, committing additional resources to these institutions to help them better prepare their students. Most of these activities have been instituted so recently that sufficient time has not passed to evaluate their effectiveness.

In targeting early adolescents, Alabama State University conducts a partnership program with local high schools that targets ninth-graders interested in teaching. The students are provided with remedial services, guidance in curriculum selection, and test-taking skills to better prepare them for college.

South Carolina has one of the most organized statewide recruitment programs operating through its Teacher Recruitment Center. Its central activity is to interest talented students in teaching. Finding minority students with high academic achievement is a top priority for its Teacher Cadet Program. High school juniors and seniors with a B+ or better average take a course on teaching, have field experiences that introduce them to a range of of teaching opportunities, and take a close look at the challenges and rewards of the teaching profession. The course is offered with support from college teacher education faculty. The Cadet Program has grown from 28 high schools serving 400 students in 1986-87 to 55 high schools and 900 students in 1987-88.

The Maryland Teacher Education and Certification Office helps local school districts, colleges, and universities build local chapters of Future Teachers of America. These chapters encourage young minority students to enter teaching. A statewide network to support the chapters is being developed and several individual schools and districts are moving ahead in establishing chapters.

In a unique venture, Los Angeles, California, Unified School District has a magnet school in a predominantly Black neighborhood that prepares high school students for teaching careers. In addition to pedagogical instruction, the students receive teaching experience.

Fiscal Support for Improving Participation. In an effort to ensure that minority high school graduates have full access to higher education in general, and teacher education in particular, a few states support programs that provide financial and other assistance to interested students. One challenge is to offer amounts large enough to lure students away from more prestigious and potentially more lucrative careers.

The Public School Forum of North Carolina's Project Teach encourages Black and American Indian high school students to consider teaching as a career and to apply for a North Carolina Teaching Fellowship to finance their college educations. The Teaching Fellows Program is a loan forgiveness plan that provides $5,000 per year for up to four years of college in exchange for up to four years of teaching after graduation. Project Teach, which started in fall 1987, employs community-based teams who carry information about the fellowship to students and parents. The teams also expose students to what is necessary to get into and stay in college, such as standardized test-taking skills and guidance counseling.

In summer 1987, Florida's Department of Education asked the legislature to double its promising teacher scholarships program to allow each high school to be eligible for two awards, one of which would be earmarked for a minority student. If there are minority students at each of Florida's eligible secondary schools, 317 scholarships would be available to minority students.

Beginning in the fall of 1987, the Georgia advisory committee funded a pilot program through Georgia Southern College to identify high school students interested in teacher education, provide them with financial and academic assistance to get into the college, and social support once they are on campus. Georgia Southern is a traditionally white institution that has suffered high attrition rates among Black students. The social support aspect of the program responds to reports that for Blacks, a key factor in attrition from the college of teacher education has been their sense of alienation from campus life.

Supporting Schools that Minorities Attend. South Carolina's historically Black colleges and universities received state funding from the 1987 legislature to cultivate qualified teacher candidates from Black high school students with average and below-average grades, primarily from small and rural school districts.

Governor James G. Martin's North Carolina Consortium to Improve Teacher Education has made a commitment to improve the preparation of Black teacher candidates. The consortium made a one-time grant of $700,000 in 1987 to the state's historically Black colleges and universities to purchase computers and National Teachers' Examination software. This effort is intended to improve the pass rates of these candidates on the state teacher exam.

Florida is considering pilot programs at community colleges where minority students are highly represented. The programs would recruit, provide initial training, and increase the retention of students who would then be eligible for teaching scholarships for their upper division coursework. This proposal presumes an increase in the two-year to four-year articulation of minority students at community and junior colleges.

Immediate Strategies. For the most part, the programs and activities described above represent long-term commitments to preparing minority students for teaching careers. Whether grooming intermediate and high school students or providing financial assistance and social support to college students, the outcomes of these practices will not be seen for at least five years. Several states have such a shortfall of qualified minority teachers and so few students in the pipeline, that more immediate action should be instituted as well. One possible solution is to develop pools of minority professionals to be brought into teaching.

The Florida legislature recently received a recommendation from the State Department of Education to declare a critical shortage of minority teachers. In so doing, funds would be available for retraining candidates drawn from alternative pools of professionals, and for scholarships, loan reimbursements, and summer institute training of high school students.

The South Carolina Teacher Recruitment Center has made alternative pool recruitment one of its goals for 1987-88. The Center hopes to recruit minorities from business and the military, both in and outside of South Carolina, for alternative route certification in critical shortage areas. A summer program to prepare alternative pool candidates for the professional standards section of the state teacher certification examination is under consideration.

Maryland's Teacher Recruitment Office has a well-developed military recruitment and preparation program targeted at three military bases in its state. At Fort Meade, for example, a teacher certification program has been designed by two institutions of higher education and delivered to officers before retirement who wish to pursue second careers in the classroom. Approximately a dozen minority military personnel and their dependents participate. In addition, the recruitment office is involved in a collaborative project that reaches out to early retirees from government and private industry. It has approached government laboratories and research centers, utility companies, and manufacturers as sources of math and science teachers. Much of the publicity in both the military and government/private industry campaigns is directed to attracting minorities.

THE REGIONAL TASK FORCE

The preceding examples were selected from a survey limited to fifteen states. No doubt other important experiments are being tried in other states, though our information suggests these tend usually to be pilot or local programs. The five task-force states involved in the SEF/NGA project set out to build on these kinds of examples, but within a framework of planning for comprehensive, statewide action.

Delegates to the regional task force reflected the diversity and variety of players and power centers within the educational decision-making processes of the states involved. Some states sent policy specialists from the governor's office; others sent key members of state legislatures, state department of education officials, and/or members of boards of education or higher education. A college president, the dean of a major graduate school of education, and members of SEF's own education advisory committee added to the mix.

Each state's delegates accepted as their charge responding to the Carnegie Report's call for state-level policies to address the minority teacher shortage, on a state-by-state level. The Regional Task Force meetings were set up to facilitate the local planning processes by examining existing state policies and initiatives, considering new ideas, and exploring the political strategies that would be required to implement new state policies successfully. No monolithic strategy or model was sought. Rather, the delegates were encouraged to take from the Regional Task Force's deliberations those ideas and strategies that lent themselves most effectively to getting the job done in their states.

Nonetheless, the opportunity to hear from experts about what was already happening in some forward-looking states, and to talk to each other about what was already going on in their respective states, inevitably produced some shared strategies as well as some individualistic ideas that fit the experience and needs of only one of the states. A look at these various shared and individual strategies will perhaps provide the best evidence of how far the group progressed in a relatively short span of time.

SHARED STRATEGIES

Not surprisingly, about half of the specific strategies developed through this process have been adopted in one form or another by more than one state. Examples include Teacher Cadet programs, "forgivable" college loans and fellowships for people who make commitments to teach in certain areas and/or certain fields, Young Educator clubs that give greater emphasis to minority participation, and Teacher Recruitment campaigns that pursue a similar emphasis.

Forgivable Loans and Fellowships

Tennessee plans to design and initiate a new Teaching Fellows Service Award Program to provide fellowships for minority students, which would include a pay-back arrangement based on teaching service within the state. Colleges and universities participating as Teaching Fellow sites would incorporate a variety of specific training experiences and mentoring relationships in their program. (Virginia, North Carolina, and Georgia have also developed variations of this kind of program.)

Teacher Cadet Programs

Virginia would create a variation on the Teacher Cadet model, specifically targeted at the middle school student. Teacher Cadet programs (also slated for Arkansas, Georgia, and Tennessee) recruit academically able secondary students to study the skills of teaching, observe master teachers, tutor younger students, and enter into mentor relationships with successful teachers.

Young Educator/Future Teacher Clubs

Arkansas proposes to develop a statewide program of Future Teacher clubs to encourage minority students and others to consider teaching, to take the necessary precollegiate academic work, and to tutor other students. Georgia and Tennessee plan variations on this model, with features designed to increase the number of minority students preparing for college, to improve their capacity to complete test requirements for entry into teacher education programs, and to assist school systems in geographic locations that have difficulty in attracting new teachers to "grow their own" teachers for future needs.

Statewide Recruitment Campaigns for the Teaching Profession

The North Carolina Initiative on the Supply of Minority Teachers seeks to encourage persons to enter or reenter the teaching profession through a variety of methods, including (1) establishing multiethnic advisory committees at both state and local levels to assist in recruiting minorities; (2) involving the media, civic and community organizations, and industry in recruiting minorities for the teaching profession; (3) identifying competent minority students as prospective teachers; and (4) providing widened exposure to teacher education programs. Virginia will design a series of programs to enhance the image of the teaching profession and encourage talented young people to consider a teaching career.

Revised Certification Regulations

Arkansas will explore alternative certification as a way to encourage adults who did not originally prepare to be teachers to become teachers. Virginia will identify the elements of certification that may have a negative impact on the supply of qualified teachers and will devise effective alternatives to these regulations.

Statewide Teacher Job Banks

Tennessee will (1) invite local school systems to list open teaching positions, (2) encourage teachers searching for positions to place resumes on file, (3) enhance the ability of qualified minority teachers to respond to the competitive environment, (4) track the placement of minority graduates from in-state teacher education programs, and (5) seek private funds to support recruitment incentives that will attract minority Tennesseans trained out of state back to the state to teach. Virginia proposes to establish a job-matching service as part of a broader state support system.

Publicize Teacher Recruitment Initiatives Among Minority Students

Two states propose to make extra efforts to stimulate increased participation of minority students in programs already in place. The Georgia task force will provide more publicity regarding funds available to students interested in teaching in critical teaching fields. North Carolina will utilize an extensive financial incentive structure already in place to increase the number of minorities entering teaching.

Improve Data Collection and Analysis

Georgia and Arkansas will take steps to improve the quality of available information about the supply of minority teachers, the minority composition of the current teaching force, and the attitudes of prospective students toward careers in teaching.

INDIVIDUAL STRATEGIES

Tennessee's task force agenda calls for the establishment of transition programs that would function as a bridge between high school and college by providing ways for minority high school students to become acculturated to the expectations of college life, in an "Upward Bound" experience for prospective teachers. Programs for members of minority groups who are presently teacher aides, substitute teachers, or community college students, but do not hold four-year degrees would be established through a matching grant program to consortia of local school systems and higher education institutions. Tennessee would also establish a matching grant program to attract minority candidates for teacher education from among graduates of four-year colleges who hold credentials in fields other than education. A separate state incentive grant program would reward higher education institutions for dealing with minority students' problems of entry, retention, and completion, and would require institutions to indicate their ability to respond to the needs of this population in the areas of curriculum, advising, mentoring, tutoring, enrichment, financial support, and counseling.

Virginia proposes to establish and staff a continuing statewide support system. The staff would administer the cadet program, a high school teacher mentor program, a college/university freshman and sophomore career seminar, a job-matching service, career-switcher programs, and a variety of other initiatives. Virginia also proposes, through a competitive grant process, to reward institutions of higher education that restructure their strategies for recruiting and retaining minority students.

Georgia plans new programs designed to increase the financial resources available to prospective minority teachers. In one, the state would encourage and stimulate the development of business-education partnerships designed to increase the private financial assistance available to future minority teachers. A second would extend an existing loan-forgiveness program currently available to college juniors and seniors to minority freshmen and sophomores.

Finally, Arkansas proposes to relate current efforts to upgrade the curriculum in the schools more directly to efforts to increase the pool of potential minority teachers, by, for example, providing in-service training to counselors on how to encourage minority students to take college prep courses and on the importance of increasing student awareness of all the options available.

IMPLEMENTATION AND FUNDING

Each state delegation accepted the responsibility for developing an implementation plan dealing with the practical issues of getting its recommendations accepted in the policy arena, and seeking sufficient financial support for those elements of each state plan that require additional expenditures. To this end, continuing state task forces on the supply of minority educators were established, drawing from a broad spectrum of the business, political, and educational communities. These task forces are assuming the responsibility, in the words of the Virginia report, for the "variety of actions necessary to further conceptualize and implement" the policy agendas such as "comprehensive data gathering, policy formation, political and private support, and organizational and agencies' approval."

Methods for funding the various state plans were developed simultaneously with the creation of their content. The North Carolina delegation, for example, decided to introduce during the "short session" of its General Assembly a bill "proposing allocation of State dollars to programs that will increase the supply of minority teachers" through the implementation of new proposals in the areas of teacher recruitment, academic preparation, and financial incentives.

Virginia, on the other hand, chose to submit a budget addendum request for support of a new program, dubbed Project TREE (Teacher Recruitment for Excellence in Education). Georgia, in addition to seeking support for certain of its proposals (e.g., Future Teachers clubs and/or Teacher Cadet programs, increased funding for minority student loans) through requests in the FY '90 budget, also decided to promote private sector initiatives through local partnership arrangements with the business community. The immediate goal of these arrangements would be to increase private financial assistance to minority students interested in becoming teachers.

CONCLUSION

As the above summary should make clear, each state that was involved in the Regional Task Force managed to make very specific, concrete progress toward the implementation of a statewide plan to deal with the issue of the declining minority teaching force, in a relatively short span of time. Why was this so?

One explanation may lie simply in the process of frequently meeting with colleagues from other states to compare notes and report progress to each other. In addition to the obvious advantages of learning from each other, this process may have imposed an urgency within each state's task force to make some concrete progress before the next regional get-together in the next state capital. These meetings, occurring on a monthly basis, thus may have helped to speed up the process as well as to infuse it with ideas from outside experts and colleagues from other states.

Another spur to progress may have derived from the willingness of local educational policymakers to look to other states (rather than, for example, to federal demonstrations or university initiatives) as major sources of new ideas. Although several observers of American education have noted a shift in the locus of innovation and initiative to the states during the Reagan years, there are still relatively few mechanisms by which one state can readily learn from another in this area. The Regional Task Force provided such a structure.

Finally, the existence of an outside agency (or, in this case, two outside agencies) willing to help facilitate the discourse among states proved very helpful. The Southern Education Foundation and the National Governors' Association not only provided the funds needed to get the delegates together on a regular basis, but also provided staff to facilitate the meetings, research current innovations, and help drive the process forward. These practical supports proved, according to many of the delegates, crucial to their ability to make rapid progress within their respective states.

4. RECRUITING AND RETAINING MINORITY TEACHERS: WHAT TEACHER EDUCATORS CAN DO

by Jody Daughtry

The demographics of our public school population are changing. Minorities constitute a higher percentage of total enrollment than ever before in our nation's history. Nationally, between 1976 and 1984, the Asian student population increased by over 85 percent and the number of Hispanic students increased by 28 percent (6, p. 64). In large urban school systems, the changes have been particularly dramatic. Boston, Denver, Portland, San Diego, and Seattle, for example, doubled their percentage of minority students between 1970 and 1982. New York, Los Angeles, Chicago, Philadelphia, Detroit, and Houston are among the many cities in the United States where minority students represent at least 75 percent of total public school enrollment. Of the nation's 20 largest public school districts, 13 are composed predominantly of minority students (6, p. 179).

When populations change, the institutions that serve them must also change. With the percentage of minority students rising, the need for minority teachers is becoming increasingly urgent. If school systems across the country that serve large numbers of minority students are to remain viable, they must increase the number of minority teachers, and they must do it quickly. The current status of minority teachers, obstacles to increasing minority participation in the teaching profession, and possible means for overcoming these obstacles are the focus of this chapter. Special attention is devoted to ways in which teacher educators at colleges and universities can help to ensure that schools will have the minority teachers who are so important to the future of public education.

CURRENT STATUS

Recent data compiled by the National Education Association (9, p. 74) indicate that about 10 percent of all teachers in the public schools are members of minority groups, while minority students represent about 29 percent of our total public school student population (6, p. 64). In areas of the country where minority student enrollment is particularly high, the figures are even more dramatic. In California, for example, about 50 percent of the students are members of minority groups, yet only 18 percent of the teachers are minorities (2).

While the disparity between the number of minority teachers and the number of minority students is great at present, the prognosis for the future is even worse. It has been estimated that by the year 2000, only 8 percent of the nation's teachers will be minorities (5, p. iii). Thus, in the next 15 years as the percentage of minority students rises, the percentage of minority teachers is predicted to decrease.

OBSTACLES TO INCREASING THE MINORITY TEACHING POOL

The low representation of minorities in the teaching ranks has been viewed as a result of both adverse socioeconomic factors and inadequate instruction at all levels of schooling, leading to fewer minority graduates at both the high school and college levels. The predicted decrease in the percentage of minority teachers, however, has been attributed to the increased use of competency tests in the field of teaching (5, p. iii). As of 1987, 45 states had adopted competency testing for initial certification of teachers and 31 states had required students to pass standardized tests for admission to teacher preparation programs (7, p. 70). Several states are also using competency tests for continuing certification. Nationally, the success rate for whites on these tests is approximately 86 percent, while the success rate for minorities is only 26 percent (4, p. 47). In spite of the undeniable differential impact of these tests on minorities versus nonminorities, the courts have upheld their use. In short, the use of competency testing presents a formidable barrier to Blacks, Asian-Americans, American Indians, and Hispanics entering the teaching profession, and no legal relief is likely to be forthcoming.

Other obstacles to equitable representation in the education profession include the high dropout rate of minorities at the high school level and the underrepresentation of minorities in the general college population. Resident minorities represented about 15 percent of enrollment at four-year institutions and about 22 percent at two-year institutions in 1986 (8, p. 170). Still another reason for the decline in the supply of minority educators is that academically talented minority students are increasingly choosing to enter fields other than teaching.

SOLUTIONS TO THE PROBLEM

In spite of the obstacles that have been outlined, there are many avenues to increasing minority participation in the teaching profession.

First, minorities can be vigorously recruited to teacher preparation programs. Potential minority teachers should be sought not only among university students, but among community college, high school, and junior high school students, as well as among adults. These individuals should be made aware of the intrinsic rewards of teaching, the high demand for teachers, recent improvements in teachers' salaries, and opportunities for advancement to supervisory and administrative positions.

Prospective Black, Asian and Pacific Islander, American Indian/Alaska Native, and Hispanic teachers can be recruited from the ranks of university students currently pursuing other majors. Programs that involve these students in tutoring can expose them to the rewards of teaching and, in many cases, cause them to change their career goals.

Posters, booklets, and other materials can be prepared for secondary schools and community colleges with high concentrations of minority students to orient both the students and their parents to the profession of teaching. Professional education faculty can be given support, especially in the form of released time and travel funds, to visit high schools and community colleges to talk directly with students about the teaching profession and to work with counselors and teachers who can play a key role in attracting and advising minority students who might be interested in teaching. Minority students who are presently preparing to be teachers can also be enlisted to help in recruitment efforts. Minority members of educational service clubs or honorary societies are usually very willing to talk with younger students about the profession. Clubs for future teachers at the secondary level can also help to foster and maintain interest in teaching.

Community organizations of various minority groups can provide an excellent forum for presenting the benefits of a career in teaching to adults. Financial incentives such as scholarships and forgivable loans for talented minority individuals who plan to enter teaching are a powerful aid to recruitment efforts. More incentives such as these are needed along with more effective dissemination of information about existing financial aid.

Beyond recruitment of minority students, efforts must also be made to ensure that those students who wish to be teachers are admitted to teacher education programs, retained, graduated, and certified. This will involve the provision of a variety of services.

Steps can be taken to identify students with potential problems in their freshman and sophomore years. When necessary, remedial instruction can be offered in basic academic skills such as reading and writing. Early exposure to and practice in taking tests similar to those needed to enter teacher education programs and to become certified can be provided. For those students who lack test-taking skills, direct instruction in this area can be given. Students can learn skills such as how to interpret test questions, how to complete tests on time, and how to guess intelligently.

Faculty, not only from schools and departments of education but also from every other academic department, need to become involved in assisting minority education students. Workshops can be given to make them aware of the content of the tests the students will be taking, what the common areas of deficiency are, how to incorporate test content into existing course objectives and content, and how to write challenging examinations that will give students the opportunity to test their knowledge.

Financial, academic, and personal counseling

available to minority students can also be improved. To supplement the counseling available to all students, minority peer advisors can be hired to provide assistance to fellow students. In addition, faculty mentors can be assigned to ensure that each minority education student receives personal help and encouragement throughout his or her program.

Finally, education faculty can provide positive minority role models. Schools and departments of education without such role models could give high priority to hiring minority faculty and could use minority adjunct faculty as well.

In addition to ensuring that minority students become certified, measures should be taken to ensure that they are hired, retained, and promoted. Placement procedures can be developed to assure that school districts seeking to hire minority teachers are put in contact with minority applicants. Assistance programs for novice teachers can be developed cooperatively by school districts and universities to reduce the attrition rate of new teachers, especially new minority teachers. Such programs can provide many types of aid. New teachers can be mentored by outstanding veteran teachers. Mentor teachers can be paid for their services and both new and mentor teachers can be periodically released from their classrooms to permit classroom observations and other types of professional development activities. Support groups can be formed for new teachers to alleviate feelings of isolation and to facilitate collective problem solving. University faculty and school district personnel can conduct workshops for new teachers on areas of common concern such as how to manage time effectively and how to cope with paperwork.

These services should increase minority graduates' chances of being hired and retained. To increase minority teachers' chances for promotion, fellowships and loans can be provided for those who wish to pursue advanced degrees.

To carry out activities such as those just described, colleges, universities, and school districts need formal, well-coordinated programs that are adequately funded and staffed by professionals. A number of such programs have been implemented around the country. For example, University of Arkansas at Pine Bluff has established the Advocacy Center for Equity and Excellence in Teacher Education to help alleviate the current and future shortage of Black teachers (1); Virginia Commonwealth University in Richmond, Virginia, has instituted a program for recruiting and mentoring minority education students (10); and fifteen school districts in California have initiated pilot projects for assisting new teachers aimed at increasing retention rates for minority as well as nonminority teachers (3, p. 4). Research should be conducted on the effectiveness of such programs and the findings disseminated so that other institutions can adopt those practices that have proved to be successful.

It is clear that much can be done to increase the number of minority teachers in the nation's public schools and that teacher educators have an important role to play in this effort. Equitable representation of minorities in the teaching profession has always been desirable; now it is a practical necessity. Minority teachers are needed to ensure that all schools are truly multicultural in perspective and that minority students have appropriate role models. Above all, minority teachers are needed if the reality of the public schools is to match the promise of democracy.

REFERENCES

1. Antonelli, G. "The Revitalization of Teacher Education at UAPB." *Action in Teacher Education 7,* no. 3 (1985)*:* 63–64.

2. California State Department of Education. *Fingertip Facts on Education in California.* Sacramento: California State Department of Education, 1988.

3. Commission on Teacher Credentialing and State Department of Education. *Draft Vignettes of Fifteen Pilot Projects: California New Teacher Project.* Sacramento: the Commission, August 1988. (Available from Commission on Teacher Credentialing, Box 944270, Sacramento, CA 94244-2700.)

4. Cooper, C. C. "Strategies to Assure Certification and Retention of Black Teachers." *The Journal of Negro Education* 55, no. 1 (1986): 46-55.

5. Goertz, M. E., and Pitcher, B. *The Impact of NTE Use by States on Teacher Selection.* Princeton, NJ: Educational Testing Service, 1985.

6. National Center for Education Statistics. *The Condition of Education.* Washington, DC: U.S. Government Printing Office, 1987.

7. _____. *The Condition of Education.* Washington, DC: U.S. Government Printing Office, 1988a.
8. _____. *The Digest of Education Statistics.* Washington, DC: U.S. Government Printing Office, 1988b.
9. National Education Association. *Status of the American Public School Teacher: 1985-86.* Washington, DC: the Association, 1987. (Available from NEA Professional Library, P.O. Box 509, West Haven, CT 06516.)
10. Reed, D. F. "Wanted: More Black Teacher Education Students." *Action in Teacher Education* 8, no. 1 (1986): 31-36.

5. MINORITY TEACHER RECRUITMENT AND RETENTION: A POTENTIAL SOLUTION TO A NATIONAL PROBLEM

by Gay C. Neuberger, Evangie H. McGlon, and Wanda M. Johnson

INTRODUCTION

Much has been written recently about minority recruitment and retention concerns at universities in general and in colleges of education in particular [see, for example, Carnegie Forum on Education and the Economy (5), Clewell and Ficklen (6), Cole (7), The Holmes Group (15), Middleton and Mason (19), National Commission for Excellence in Teacher Education (20), and Orum (23)]. In the following pages, we present an as yet hypothetical model for a minority recruitment and retention program, Accent on Teacher Education Experiences for Minorities (A-TEEM), whose features draw from the literature and from our experience with minority recruitment and retention. With these sources of information in mind, we have tried to go beyond the many now-familiar ideas about minority recruitment and retention to create an academic program that confronts the problem by significantly broadening the base of potential minority talent that might become involved in education. A-TEEM accomplishes this broadening through identification of a diverse group of positions that can be defined as encompassing teaching roles, developing university programs that prepare minorities to assume these positions, and then formalizing the ensuing educational accomplishments with the issuance of university certificates or degrees, as appropriate.

It should be noted that although this chapter does point out a number of support elements that would be needed for students' success in the academic program, we do not attempt to address all of the questions and considerations involved in developing a program of this type. Furthermore, the A-TEEM concept, as presented herein, is still in the conceptualization phase and has yet to be tested within any actual university setting.

A-TEEM: ACCENT ON TEACHER EDUCATION EXPERIENCES FOR MINORITIES

The goal of A-TEEM is to involve as many minorities as possible in educational endeavors in a variety of settings. A-TEEM is designed to enhance recruitment of minorities into colleges of education, and hence, the teaching profession, and then to maximize the probability that these students will complete their university programs and assume the various teaching positions for which they were educated.

The centerpiece of the A-TEEM program is an array of teaching preparation programs that are available to minority students. These programs offer the opportunity to spend time ranging from a minimum of two semesters to the period required to obtain full teacher certification in pursuit of college studies aimed at enhancing the educations of young people. By providing preparation for a range of teaching careers, A-TEEM appeals to a potentially large pool of minority students. As a result of this program, it would be possible to place significant numbers of minorities in a variety of educational settings where they can provide role models for young people while enjoying satisfying careers.

The chapter begins with a brief description of the several A-TEEM certificate and degree programs. This is followed by a discussion of the broadened base of minority students toward whom A-TEEM recruitment efforts would be directed. And finally, the chapter provides a sketch of the institutional setting and resources that would be required to implement the A-TEEM model.

A-TEEM ACADEMIC PROGRAMS

In coordination with other colleges in the university, area vocational-technical schools, and commu-

---

The authors wish to thank Dr. Kay Sather Bull and Dr. Michael M. Warner for their suggestions and feedback on an earlier version of this chapter.

nity organizations, a college of education that implemented the A-TEEM program would offer A-TEEM and other interested students the opportunity to prepare for a variety of careers that feature teaching as the central experience. These career opportunities differ in a number of respects, including (a) required prior educational experiences, (b) required amount of college preparation, (c) resulting certification and licensure, and (d) income that can be anticipated on program completion. The following academic program description groups the study options by ages of students with whom an A-TEEM participant might plan to work.

Programs for Working with Young Children

With the increase in working two-parent and single-parent families, there is a great need for increased available quality care for infants, toddlers, and young children. A-TEEM believes that quality care involves more than meeting the nutritional, cleanliness, and safety needs of children. Because a child's later academic success depends on receipt of sufficient and appropriate pre-academic experiences during the first years of life, this too is part of quality care. A-TEEM would offer a two-semester program to prepare caretakers in day care or private home settings to provide age-appropriate, academic readiness activities. Coursework would include content covering normal and abnormal early child development, instructional materials in the daily environment, nutrition, and normal and abnormal communication skills (ages birth through 7 years). All coursework would have major observation/participation components followed by class discussion. Minority students who have completed at least three years of high school and reached the age of 24 years are eligible for this program. A certificate of completion is awarded at the end of the program.

To formally prepare persons having some previous college credit to assume several of a teacher's classroom responsibilities in the elementary grades, A-TEEM students might enroll in a three-semester program for teachers' aides. Those who complete this program would be qualified to work in a regular classroom under the direct supervision of the teacher. Preparation to work as an aide with moderately or severely handicapped students requires a fourth semester of college courses. Certificates of completion are issued at the end of both programs.

For those who wish to pursue a bachelor's degree in preparation for working with young children, A-TEEM would continue to offer traditional degree programs leading to certification in nursery school and kindergarten teaching. The bachelor's degree in elementary education would qualify students for a license to teach kindergarten through eighth grade.

Programs for Working with Adolescents

A variety of structured youth recreational programs could benefit from leadership by adults with knowledge of how to make leisure-time activities more educational. Scouting, park district programs, fitness and sports groups, social clubs, YMCAs and YWCAs, and 4-H programs, for example, offer programs that would be enhanced by having adult leaders who are sensitive to the educational implications of each organization's traditional activities and skilled in transforming these activities into educational experiences. Through A-TEEM, two-to-four semester programs for persons at least 24 years of age with a minimum of three years of high school would award certificates of completion for preparation in the educational underpinnings and methods of working in such areas as the visual and performing arts, sports and recreational activities, homemaking, handicrafts, nature studies, health and nutrition concepts, animal care, and community service. Persons who complete this program also would be eligible for positions as club/activity sponsors in secondary schools, thereby relieving teachers of this noninstructional drain on their time.

Minorities with some college credit can enroll in an A-TEEM program to prepare as teachers' aides at the secondary level. This three-semester program includes coursework in one or two content areas selected by the student, as well as introductory pedagogical methods. On completion of the program, aides would receive a certificate of completion and would be qualified to work under the direct supervision of a secondary classroom teacher.

A-TEEM also would offer the traditional bachelor's degree in secondary education in a variety of disciplines. Successful program completion would qualify the student for a secondary license.

Programs for Working with Adults

For students holding a high school diploma or the equivalent, A-TEEM would offer a two-semester program to prepare them to work in various clerical positions in an elementary or secondary school. In addition to coursework in typing/word processing, duplicating equipment, and office procedures, students would be provided with content on the structure of the school and the roles of its various employees, the role of schools in American society, and child/adolescent development. This program awards a certificate of completion.

As information emerges on the high rate of functional illiteracy in the United States, many communities are establishing adult literacy programs to correct this problem. Through A-TEEM, students with some college credit might enroll in a two-semester program that prepares them to work with adults who want to learn to read, write, and compute. A-TEEM students also would receive instruction in adult development and characteristics of adult learners. A certificate of completion is awarded at the end of this program.

And finally, for those minorities who are bilingual and have earned some college credit, A-TEEM has a two-semester program to prepare them to work in communities in need of instructors in English as a Second Language (ESL). This program provides coursework in ESL methods; child, adolescent, and adult development; characteristics of adult learners; and cross-cultural perspectives on American life. It results in a certificate of completion.

Whereas the ideal would be to enroll as many A-TEEM students as possible in programs leading to full teacher licensure, in practice, limiting the available programs in this way greatly limits minority participation in colleges of education and the teaching profession. It is anticipated that some who initially enroll in A-TEEM certificate of completion programs will later return to complete full teacher certification programs.

A-TEEM STUDENTS

The competition within and between universities to recruit qualified minorities to the various disciplines and professions is becoming increasingly stiff since de jure and de facto segregation have been all but eliminated and most universities and employers now find themselves in serious need of improving their records on minority enrollment and hiring. Realistically, colleges of education presently are not highly competitive in the recruitment arena when per capita funding of the colleges themselves is seriously deficient, and when salaries for program graduates are well below the minimum appropriate for the amount of education completed by teachers, the intensity of the work, and the inherent responsibility entrusted to teachers by society for the futures of our youth.

However, all is not lost for education. Unlike many of the more lucrative professions that have very few capacities in which one might be fully involved as an active professional, there are a great number of positions that inherently involve teaching. Several of these positions are ones for which A-TEEM offers formal instruction and that can be filled appropriately by people having a wide range of academic preparation. This being the case, the pool of possible minority students available for recruitment into colleges of education is potentially vast. This section describes several of the population segments from which a college of education might recruit for A-TEEM.

Junior High School Future Teachers

When students enter college knowing their academic and vocational goals, this is often because a respected relative or friend of the family has served as a role model (e.g., the family physician), and/or because the students have had some opportunity to practice and enjoy work related to a given vocation (e.g., through summer employment). In disadvantaged communities with large minority populations, however, positive career role models may be in short supply.

Although some minority students overcome such beginnings, many do not without assistance. Therefore, an A-TEEM program would sponsor Futures in

Teaching (FIT), an enrichment program to help young minority students become interested in careers in teaching.

FIT provides an array of experiences for junior high school students and their teachers to help the young people become focused on teaching as a career. Working in schools with large minority enrollments, FIT personnel from the college of education offer in-service programs and on-campus workshops to alert teachers (a) to the need for more minority teachers, and (b) to ways of working with prospective candidates beginning at a young age, including through organization of junior high school tutoring programs.

For the students, FIT offers seminars on careers in teaching tailored to the junior high level. Some seminars are held in the schools, but occasionally groups of students are brought to the university campus for weekend workshops during which they attend presentations/discussions, meet college of education faculty, and tour college and other facilities. One- to two-week summer "teaching camps" on the university campus provide rudimentary pedagogical instruction, including methods, materials, and practice aimed at improvement of tutoring performance.

Nontraditional Students

One of the fastest growing segments of the college student population is that group known as nontraditional students (18). Typically, they are defined by some combination of chronological age (those who are at least 24 or 25 years of age) and/or social role (e.g., a single 18-year-old with two children) and/or enrollment pattern (e.g., evening or part-time students) (18, 24). They include displaced homemakers, single parents, dislocated workers, and workers seeking changes from nonacademically oriented careers.

Census data from 1986 indicate that 17 percent of college enrollees were Black or of Hispanic origin. Of these minority students, 18 percent (539,000) were in the 25- to 34-year-old age group (28). This makes the older minority population a potentially rich source of recruits.

Nontraditional students return to school for a variety of personal and vocational reasons, including vocational updating, midlife career changes, or preparation to embark on a first career (17). Whatever the reasons for returning, these older students as a group are looking for programs to meet a variety of interests and needs, only some of which may require a full traditional four- or five-year undergraduate degree (10). With its array of education-related program options, an A-TEEM program would make a college of education very attractive to this expanding group of potential students.

Teachers' Aides

Currently employed teachers' aides constitute a readily identifiable group with a demonstrated interest in teaching. Some may have considered the possibility of becoming fully licensed teachers and rejected the notion as being unrealistic. Others may not yet have thought about it. Special emphasis during all initial A-TEEM presentations to teachers' aides would be on a realistic discussion of the feasibility of meeting college and university entrance requirements and of obtaining adequate financial assistance.

Traditional College Enrollees

The A-TEEM concept offers a full range of education career opportunities to people with a variety of backgrounds, interests, and abilities. As such, the program seeks to enroll a diverse group of students. This group includes the largest possible number of the most talented and well-prepared minority students graduating from the nation's high schools. These traditional college enrollees will eventually assume the bulk of the fully licensed teaching positions held by minorities. For reasons of equity and development of minority teacher role models in the schools who can positively influence the lives of many young people over the years, successful recruitment and retention of these top students are vital. The remainder of this section deals with several factors related to recruitment and retention of the traditional undergraduate minority education major.

Recruitment. Colleges and universities focus special student recruitment efforts on a variety of identifiable student populations, only one of which is minorities (e.g., athletes, honors students, the handicapped, those destined for careers in science, nontraditional students). Our present concern would be to develop a recruitment program that enables not only whites, but also Blacks, Hispanics, Asians and Pacific Islanders, and American Indians/Alaska Natives to learn about the availability and accessibility of a high-quality undergraduate teacher preparation program at the A-TEEM university. The recruitment program must first find its audience and then sell the idea that participation in A-TEEM is a realistic goal.

Traditionally there are three major audiences for A-TEEM recruitment efforts into the teacher education program leading to full licensure. These are:

1. *High schools with large minority populations.* Beginning as early as ninth grade, promising minority students would be identified by the A-TEEM recruiter, and their progress through the high school years would be monitored.

2. *Junior colleges.* At some universities, there is already is a well-established pattern of receiving transfer students from junior colleges. Since large numbers of minorities begin their postsecondary educations in two-year colleges (23), this makes these feeder institutions a potentially rich source of minority teacher candidates.

3. *Undecided majors.* These already-enrolled university students may constitute a sizable audience for A-TEEM recruitment. Because these students already would have made the initial decision to enroll at the university, recruiting efforts could concentrate on what a career in teaching might offer them.

The A-TEEM minority recruiter will be asked to address a number of student concerns about entering teaching. In addition to the usual questions about teachers' salaries, two of the major concerns are likely to be about ability to meet the rising academic standards in the field of education (a question involving assessment practices) and ability to meet the rising costs of a college education (a question involving financial assistance).

At every step of the educational process, assessment practices can make the difference between success and failure for many minority students. Students with marginal assessment histories may rule themselves out of a teaching career for fear of being rejected, despite a desire to enter teaching. For those who persevere, actual rejection by the admissions office may soon follow. There is increasing recognition, however, that if an entire pool of talented teachers is not to be lost as a result of rigid adherence to a single narrow type of evaluation system, alternative measures of academic potential must be introduced into the system. While not all potential minority students will need to participate in alternative forms of assessment for admission to the university and/or college, some alternatives must be available as part of what the recruiter is able to offer.

The question of available financial assistance will loom large in the minds of prospective A-TEEM recruits. Direct (e.g., scholarships, loans) and indirect (e.g., free or low-cost housing and/or day care) financial assistance must be part of the package the recruiter can promote to interested minorities. This is true for older, nontraditional students as well as traditional enrollees (24).

Retention. Attrition of minority students enrolled in higher education is a major problem. The literature indicates that the first six weeks of the freshman year are critical to determining whether a student remains in or leaves an institution (21, 27). This is a time during which student enthusiasm and willingness to work can be either reinforced or diminished, depending on the response the student receives from the institution (4).

Retention begins with establishment of a strong institutional support base, including orientation programs that span a period of weeks rather than days. And as the weeks go by, the importance of academic advisement, counseling, and supplemental assistance cannot be overstated.

Dormitory life constitutes a major part of many undergraduate students' college experiences. Are not-so-subtle patterns of segregated room assignments creating a class system? Are rooms that are integrated by assignment rather than mutual choice filled with tension? A-TEEM personnel need to work with dormitory staff to examine the living situations for minorities in the dormitories and remediate deficiencies when they are identified.

Minority students who are expected to someday become role models for others often arrive on desegregated college campuses in need of role models themselves. Yet most desegregated campuses have so few minority students and faculty that racial/ethnic isolation can quickly set in. A goal of A-TEEM is to increase the number of minority students in the college of education to a point where this isolation is no longer a major fact of life. But peers do not usually serve as adequate role models. For this there must be sufficient minority faculty visible and accessible. One way to accomplish this is through the A-TEEM Minority Lectureship Program that brings to campus highly qualified doctoral-level minorities to teach courses in the college, meet with undergraduates, and serve as role models.

INSTITUTIONAL SETTING

The Accent on Teacher Education Experiences for Minorities program has been conceptualized for implementation by a college of education housed within a midsized to large university that offers a full array of academic programs and services, and is located in or within commuting distance of a major metropolitan area. At the time of A-TEEM implementation, it would be helpful for the college of education to be in a dynamic state that could accommodate program changes. An ideal time to introduce A-TEEM might be during the development of and transition to an extended five- or six-year teacher education program. Since this would be a period of redirection for the college, with an emphasis on qualitative improvements in the experiences of all teacher education students, the A-TEEM concept might more easily be accommodated in the new structure, even as it helps to define that structure for the teacher education curriculum.

ASSEMBLING A-TEEM RESOURCES

If a college of education is planning to make a serious effort to improve its recruitment and retention of minority students, now is the time to begin assembling the resources to support this effort. Before the first prospective minority students can be approached for A-TEEM, a number of steps must be taken to ensure a welcoming and supportive environment when the students arrive. A brief discussion of the staffing, attitudes, arrangements, and activities that combine to form the A-TEEM resources follows.

Administrative Commitment

If the effort to increase recruitment and retention of minority teachers is to succeed, higher education administrators cannot be detached from the process. They must be fully committed to A-TEEM as part of their overall commitment to a higher quality educational experience for all students. Clear administrative support has psychological benefits for all university personnel and students, plus it can make the difference between success or failure in funding A-TEEM.

Program Funding

College and university-level administrators need to realize that a commitment to the A-TEEM concept implies a substantial commitment of dollars and university resources. Direct funding is needed to provide financial assistance to students in the program, to hire, equip and house A-TEEM personnel, and to fund A-TEEM recruitment activities. Indirect funding needs arise in the form of additional academic offerings and strengthened/enhanced extant support services to accommodate the specific needs of minority students and their families.

Of special concern here is availability of funds to use for financial aid. The degree of effort devoted to providing financial aid serves as a major indicator to potential students of the college's commitment to having them on campus. The education of students is in everybody's interest, and there are a number of potential funding sources that could be tapped to form a reservoir for minority financial aid, including grants and contracts, state and federal manpower training funds, alumni, area business people, and professional groups.

Academic Coursework

On many desegregated campuses, there continues to be tension between minority students and their majority peers, as well as between faculty and minority students. This situation has long and complex origins and generally mirrors the status of race relations in society at large. An important A-TEEM component is the development of coursework and seminars with content that confronts the origins and manifestations of racial/ethnic conflict, and provides opportunities for minority and majority students to work through their differences.

Toward this end, all college of education students at an A-TEEM university are required to take coursework that highlights the contributions of minorities to various fields of study, and seminars on cultural pluralism as the concept relates to interpersonal relations at the elementary, secondary, and postsecondary school levels. Faculty workshops are offered to characterize the several minority groups represented on campus, and to clarify the fact that there are major differences between and within these groups.

Collaborative Relationships

The entire A-TEEM concept embodies a strong community outreach component. Attracting students to the program requires that A-TEEM personnel become involved with the community to an extent usually not attempted by traditional university programs. But beyond the obvious need to recruit students from the community, A-TEEM requires the formation of a number of collaborative relationships to function. Two such relationships are with area vocational-technical schools and with community organizations.

In order to avoid duplication of course offerings and reduce the costs of A-TEEM, some A-TEEM course content could be offered through the adult education division of the area vocational-technical school Such coursework might include the clerical component of the preparation for clerical positions in the schools, and much of the subject specific content (e.g., health and nutrition concepts, nature studies) in the program to prepare adult leaders for youth recreation programs.

A-TEEM looks to the surrounding community for program planning, financial assistance, and field experience sites. Community advisory groups would help answer such questions as "What programs should be developed?" and "Where are the students for these programs?" Since A-TEEM would function in part as a community job training program, it should be expected that community businesses would contribute to student financial aid fund-raising drives and also help to ensure that employment opportunities will be available when students complete their A-TEEM programs. And, finally, the nature of the instruction for many A-TEEM programs requires access to local nonprofit and for-profit community organizations for field-based observation and participation sites.

A-TEEM Personnel

A-TEEM program personnel work with minority students at several points in their educational careers and in a number of capacities. A-TEEM personnel are recruiters, advisors, teachers, and community liaisons.

Recruiter. College recruitment at its best requires the efforts of one or more designated individuals who can undertake the necessary background research, establish the personal contacts, and follow up on the inquiries and status of applicants (11, 25). The minority recruiter is responsible for identifying potential program participants, establishing contact with them to increase program visibility and respond to questions, and overseeing each prospective student's admission and financial aid applications to be sure that they are fully completed and received on time by the appropriate office(s).

Advisor. Academic advisement is an important element in any college program. It is especially so in a program such as A-TEEM, in which many of the students may be unsure about their scholastic ability and/or their educational goals. A-TEEM advisement assists students to explore goals in relation to abilities, and provides help in selection of appropriate academic programs (14). Academic advisors work with students to identify and select coursework, and develop class schedules that balance requirements and electives, as well as study time and leisure time, with the outcome that the students remain enrolled in college.

Teacher. A-TEEM personnel are required to team teach the multicultural content courses in the university. They also offer seminars and workshops to a variety of students and teachers on topics ranging from the benefits of a career in education to multicultural sensitivity.

Community Liaison. Community support for A-TEEM is essential to its success. As discussed above, reasons for this include: (a) the surrounding community is a potential source of students, (b) community business people are a potential source of program funding, and (c) community organizations and agencies can serve as observation and participation sites for students in the various teacher education programs. Responsibility for developing and maintaining community relations should be assigned to specific individuals.

University Support Services

Before A-TEEM students arrive on campus, a full complement of support services must be in place to assist them if the need arises. There must be a comprehensive orientation program to provide a complete, but not overwhelming, picture of college life in general, and the academic structuring of the university and the college in particular. Much of the college orientation is handled through the college of education Minority Mentor Program (MMP), which matches graduate minority education students with beginning education students. These graduate students serve as role models, provide information on the various options available in teacher education, act as someone with whom ideas can be discussed, and generally help the undergraduate maintain the motivation to achieve academically.

After the students have settled in at the university, many will need to focus their attention on serious vocational planning for the first time. Gordon (13) found that one characteristic of students at high risk for failing to complete college degree programs is uncertainty about their academic and vocational goals. Vocational counseling must be offered by personnel who have knowledge of vocational/career planning and background working effectively with minorities.

Extracurricular Programs

As discussed above, participants in A-TEEM would form a highly diverse group. They would range in age from the typical 18-year-old freshman to middle age. They might be single or married, living with and without their nuclear families. Some can develop their own extracurricular resources, while many others need assistance. As part of A-TEEM, the following student needs should be anticipated so the structure to meet them will be in place before the requests for assistance begin to surface.

All students need social outlets in addition to their academic experiences. A-TEEM must work with campus activity sponsors to promote inclusion of minorities in all activities, including participation in leadership roles. Like other students, minorities are interested in service work that can be a source of personal satisfaction as well as a method of building a resume. The A-TEEM Human Resource and Youth Service file maintains listings of various education- and noneducation-related service opportunities open to students on campus and in the community.

While many of the 18- to 22-year-old A-TEEM students will be interested in the types of social and service opportunities described above, older A-TEEM students will often have entirely different extracurricular needs. They may well arrive on campus with children whose needs must be met if the parents are to succeed in school; for example, low- or no-cost quality day care and evening care, tutoring during the years when parents are too busy with their own schoolwork to help their children, and supervised recreation and employment opportunities for older children. Many of these child-centered needs could be addressed by coordinating them with the needs of various college of education programs to obtain children/students for laboratory/practicum experiences.

SUMMARY AND CONCLUSIONS

We have described a hypothetical model program called Accent on Teacher Education Experiences for Minorities (A-TEEM). Although the model leaves many program details yet to be specified, we have tried to paint a broad picture of the various programmatic offerings from which a prospective student may choose, the variety of students who would be involved with A-TEEM at different points in their educational careers, the institutional framework that would be needed to support A-TEEM, and the underlying support structures that would have to be in place before A-TEEM is implemented. Of course, before any given institution can begin to formulate its plan of action, it must first examine its own "unique racial history and its efforts, or lack thereof, to enhance the opportunities for blacks [and other minorities]" (25), since specific solutions to problems must emerge from their own particular contexts.

Recruitment and retention of minorities into the teaching profession constitute a national problem. We believe that by expanding the definition of "teaching profession" to include the numerous employment opportunities that inherently involve teaching, there are a variety of useful program options that can be maximized to prepare minorities to fill teaching roles and, thereby, work to ameliorate the looming national minority teacher shortage crisis.

SELECTED REFERENCES

1. American Association of Colleges for Teacher Education. "Minority Teacher Recruitment and Retention: A Call for Action." (Unpublished) Washington, DC: AACTE, 1987.
2. Astin, A. W. *Minorities in American Higher Education.* San Franciso: Jossey-Bass, 1982.
3. Aulston, M. D. *Comparative Perceptions of the College Environment Between Minority-Group Freshmen and Minority-Entering Transfer Students.* Storrs, CT: University of Connecticut, 1972.
4. Betts, M. "Freshman Orientation: An Integrated Approach." (Unpublished) Stillwater, OK: Oklahoma State University, Office of Admissions, 1987.
5. Carnegie Forum on Education and the Economy. *A Nation Prepared: Teachers for the 21st Century.* New York: Carnegie Forum, 1986.
6. Clewell, B. C., and Ficklen, M. S. *Improving Minority Retention in Higher Education: A Search for Effective Institutional Practices.* Princeton, NJ: Educational Testing Service, 1986.
7. Cole, B. P. "The Black Educator: An Endangered Species." *Journal of Negro Education* 55, no. 3 (1986): 326-34.
8. Covert, R. W.; Fang, W. L.; Eslinger, V.; and Stump, R. J. "Evaluating Racial Attitudes: A Process for Promoting Racial Awareness." Paper presented at the second annual Conference on Minority Recruiting and Retention, Lexington, KY, January 1988.
9. Crockett, D. S. *Academic Advising: A Resource Document.* Iowa City, IA: American College Testing Program, 1978.
10. Cross, K. P. *Adults as Learners.* San Francisco: Jossey-Bass, 1981.
11. Dorsey-Gaines, C., and Lewis, B. J. "How to Start a Minority Recruitment Program: A Case Study." *The Journal of College Admissions,* no. 116 (1987): 3-6.
12. Gibbs, J. T. "Black Students at a White University: An Exploratory Study." (Unpublished) Berkeley, CA: University of California-Berkeley, School of Social Welfare, 1973.
13. Gordon, V. N. "Students with Uncertain Academic Goals." In *Increasing Student Retention,* edited by L. Noel, R. Levitz, D. Saluri, and Associates, 116-37. San Francisco: Jossey-Bass, 1987.
14. Habley, W. "Academic Advisement: The Critical Link in Student Retention." *NASPA Journal* 19 (1981): 46-49.
15. The Holmes Group. *Tomorrow's Teachers: A Report of the Holmes Group.* East Lansing, MI: Holmes Group, 1986.
16. Joseph, G. I. "Black Students on a Predominantly White Campus." *Journal of the National Association of Women Deans and Counselors* 32, no. 2 (1969): 63-66.
17. Knowles, M. S. *The Modern Practice of Adult Education: From Pedagogy to Andragogy.* Chicago: Follett, 1980.
18. Lace, W. W. "A Nontraditional Approach: Who Those Nontraditional Students Are—And Why You Should Be Interested in Them." *Currents* 12, no. 5 (1986): 8-11.
19. Middleton, E. J., and Mason, E. J., eds. *Recruitment and Retention of Minority Students in Teacher Education: Proceedings of the National Invitational Conference.* Lexington, KY: University of Kentucky, 1987.
20. National Commission for Excellence in Teacher Education. *A Call for Change in Teacher Education.* Washington, DC: American Association of Colleges for Teacher Education, 1985.
21. Noel, L. "College Student Retention—A Campus-Wide Responsibility." *National ACAC Journal* 21, no. 1 (1976): 33-36.
22. Noel, L.; Levitz, R.; Saluri, D.; and Associates, eds. *Increasing Student Retention.* San Francisco: Jossey-Bass, 1987.
23. Orum, L. S. *The Education of Hispanics: Status and Implications.* Washington, DC: National Council of La Raza, 1986.

24. Pappas, J. P., and Loring, R. K. "Returning Learners." In *Increasing Student Retention,* edited by L. Noel, R. Levitz, D. Saluri, and Associates, 138–61. San Francisco: Jossey-Bass, 1987.

25. Reisler, M. "Colleges Need Aggressive, Inspiring Leadership If They Are to Achieve Genuine Integration." *Chronicle of Higher Education* 34, no. 19 (1988): A52.

26. Salahu-Din, H. "Campus Perceptions of Students: Implications for Strategic Planning in Black Student Recruitment and Retention." *Educational Considerations* 15, no. 1 (1988): 25–30.

27. Terenzini, P. T., and Pascarella, E. T. "Voluntary Freshman Attrition and Patterns of Social and Academic Integration in a University: A Test of a Conceptual Model." *Research in Higher Education* 6 (1977): 25–43.

28. U.S. Department of Commerce, Bureau of the Census. "School Enrollments—Social and Economic Characteristics of Students." *Current Population Reports,* Series P-20, No. 429, 1986.

6. INCREASING THE POOL OF BLACK TEACHERS: PLANS AND STRATEGIES
(Norfolk State University)

by Elaine P. Witty

America's schools require the recruitment of teachers who are self-assured, competent, loving, and demanding. Included in this group must be teachers who represent the diversity of cultural and racial backgrounds presented by the students. Special efforts are needed to provide an acceptable ratio of minority teachers to minority students. This chapter presents a discussion of the issues related to increasing the number of minority teacher candidates and gives practical suggestions for strategies that may be employed.

THE CHALLENGES

Black, Asian and Pacific Islander, American Indian/Alaska Native, and Hispanic teachers are underrepresented in public school classrooms today. They are also underrepresented in teacher education programs. While Black, Hispanic, Asian-American, and American Indian students represent approximately one-third of the school population, and their numbers are increasing, teachers from these groups represent less than 10 percent of the population, and their numbers are decreasing.

A smaller percentage of the teachers in America now are Black than was the case in 1980. A recent National Education Association survey revealed that in 1986, Blacks comprised only 6.9 percent of the teaching force (12). This figure has declined from 9.7 percent reported by the National Education Association in 1980 (13).

The picture for the future does not look bright. According to the American Association of Colleges for Teacher Education (AACTE), the number of minority students enrolled in teacher education is shockingly low. Of all college students studying to become teachers, only 4.3 percent were Black, 2.5 percent were Asian, and 1.5 percent were Hispanic (3).

Although some people will enter the teaching profession through alternative certification routes, for the immediate future most Black teachers will likely enter the profession through teacher education programs. While there is an upturn in the number of white adults entering teaching through alternative certification routes, deans of schools of education at historically Black universities report that the number of Black adults following the alternative certification program is small.

Two major challenges must be addressed. First, stronger efforts must be initiated to assure success for a larger portion of college students who enroll in teacher education programs. Second, a larger number of students must be prepared and recruited into teacher education programs. Parity in the teacher-pupil ratio is necessary for sound educational programs for all pupils.

The shortage of minority teachers and advocates, and the inaccessibility of adequate minority role models add to the difficulties minority students experience in schools. Further, white pupils are denied the support and encouragement that they may need in order to learn racial tolerance, understanding, and respect for authority figures whose racial/ethnic backgrounds are different from their own. In a global world with a nonwhite majority, this failure can prove disastrous.

Improving education will benefit minority families as well as the nation. While the writers of *A Nation at Risk* (11) noted that national survival was related to educational achievement, they failed to consider the needs of the public schools with respect to the education of minority students. Demographic studies indicate that the future work force will increasingly include members of the minority population. Informed self-interest, therefore, suggests that it is essential to provide good educational training for groups that the nation will depend on for a large portion of goods and services.

RECRUITMENT PROBLEMS

The components of the problem of attracting a large pool of academically able Black students into teacher preparation programs at traditionally Black colleges and universities are complex and interrelated. The following list resulted from a review of the literature and from consultations with representatives from the five traditionally Black colleges and universities in Virginia.

1. Inadequate development of basic skills by a large percentage of minority elementary school, middle school, and high school students (7). This is an educational pipeline problem.

2. Inadequate counseling at levels of education when critical program-planning decisions are made causes a disproportionate number of Black students to go through vocational tracks rather than academic tracks in secondary school (15).

3. Lack of a positive image of teaching generally. The number of baccalaureate degrees in education conferred to Black, Hispanic, Asian-American, and American Indian students dropped 50.2 percent from 1975-76 to 1984-85 (4).

4. Insufficient encouragement by counselors, teachers, and parents for academically able students who may be interested in teaching as a career.

5. Lack of awareness in minority communities of the pending shortage of minority teachers.

6. Sensitivity to the stigma of predictions of high failure rates on the NTE and other teacher tests. Institutions such as Grambling, Norfolk State University, and the University of Arkansas at Pine Bluff have reported significant improvements in student performance on teacher tests (10, 14, 17).

7. Lack of sufficient funding of teacher education programs resulting in limited resources for recruitment.

8. Lack of enticements and attractions such as scholarships and attractive loan programs that compete with those in other fields of study. Minority students are finding that loan debts incurred during college are very difficult to repay if they are not successful in passing the barriers to teacher certification and securing employment as teachers.

RECOMMENDATIONS FOR ACTION

Since the 1982 publication of *Prospects for Black Teachers: Preparation, Certification, Employment* (19), a number of groups and professional organizations have addressed the issue of minority teacher recruitment and retention. The major reports include the following recommendations:

1. The National Commission on Excellence in Teacher Education of the American Association of Colleges for Teacher Education recommended that (1) federal and state governments, and private philanthropies should ensure that the lack of finances will not bar qualified minority students from entering teacher education programs; (2) parents, teachers, counselors, and principals should encourage minority students to consider careers in teaching; and (3) colleges and universities should provide a supportive climate; and above all, intellectually demanding teacher education programs should prepare graduates to meet certification requirements (1).

2. The Holmes Group stated that Holmes Group members should help to create a profession representative of the larger society; specifically, it proposed that members should: (1) increase recruitment at the precollege level; (2) endorse loan forgiveness programs for minority students; and (3) work to reduce the effects of handicapping conditions, poverty, race, and ethnicity on the entry to the profession (9).

It should be noted that The Holmes Group propositions are aimed at member institutions only and only one historically Black institution, Howard University, was invited to membership.

3. The Carnegie Forum on Education and the Economy gives an excellent discussion on the rationale for providing a representative number

of minority teachers and recommends the creation of a partnership of government, the private sector, the minority community, and the schools to ensure an increasing number of minority teachers. The report points out that "at the heart of the issue is the need to greatly increase the flow through the educational pipeline of members of these minority groups so they can join the pool of eligible candidates" (6).

4. The Southern Regional Educational Board recommends (1) financial incentives to attract qualified minorities into teaching, and (2) extra efforts to ensure that disadvantaged students who want to teach are prepared to meet the higher standards required for teachers (16).

Responding to the continuing decline in the number of Black teacher education students enrolled in member institutions, the AACTE released a policy statement on December 14, 1987. It proposed ten specific programs: (1) National Scholarship Program, (2) State Scholarship Program, (3) Targeted High School Work-Study Program, (4) Targeted College Work-Study Program, (5) Two-Year/Four-Year Articulation Program, (6) Assistantship and Grants Program, (7) Entry Incentive Program, (8) Support Program for Re-entry and Career Change, (9) Targeted Teacher Induction Program, and (10) Assessment Demonstration Grants Program. The AACTE announced its intentions to aggressively pursue programs and policies to assist member institutions to increase minority participation (2).

It should be noted that the recommendations by these groups have not been implemented; therefore, no evidence is available by which to gauge their impact on actually increasing the number of Black, Hispanic, Asian-American, and American Indian teachers available for public schools.

DEVELOPING RECRUITMENT PLANS

The following guidelines for developing recruitment plans were derived from a study conducted for the Division of Teacher Education and Certification in the Virginia Department of Education (18).

It is clear that certain improvements in the workplace for teachers would greatly improve the attractiveness of teaching as a career choice for high school students. Better salaries, more power in professional decisions, impoved working conditions, and greater community appreciation and respect would enhance recruitment efforts. A study by Linda Darling-Hammond (8) provides documentation of these points. The principles listed here, however, relate specifically to activities under the direct authority of institutions of higher education or public schools as they are presently operating.

1. Recruitment efforts should highlight the intrinsic rewards of a teaching career for students who express an interest in teaching.

2. Recruitment efforts should start at least as early as seventh grade. Students must be assisted in selecting the appropriate courses to earn the academic diploma. They should also be advised and assisted in enrolling in the academic tracks in high school. [Charlotte Scott, in 1982, found that of the 7,125 Black public school seniors who planned to enter colleges in Virginia, only 40 percent were enrolled in an academic program. Sixty-one percent of the white seniors who planned to go to college were in academic high school programs. A large percentage of the Black high school students who expressed interest in teaching as a career were from homes where fathers and mothers had no more than a high school education. Students in such homes tend to rely heavily on counselors for academic program planning advice. Most of these students are in vocational tracks (15)].

3. Recruitment efforts should include some form of financial assistance. The largest percentage of Black high school students who express interest in teaching as a career are from low-income families.

4. Recruitment efforts tailored to the underprepared, high-potential student should include explanations of academic support available, personalized instruction, and a peer counseling program.

5. High school guidance counselors should be included as integral parts of recruitment pro-

grams for academically able Black high school graduates. [Scott's 1982 study showed that 71 percent of the Black students, as compared to 51 percent of the white students, ranked guidance counselors as important in helping them to make educational plans (15)].

6. Special attention should be given to the subject fields where there are shortages and projected shortages of teachers. Students should be recruited especially for targeted fields. A survey of teacher placement officers identified nationwide shortages in the following fields: Mathematics, Physics, Computer Programming, Chemistry, Data Processing, Bilingual Education, Special Education, Earth Science, Biology, and English (5). Students are more attracted to the prospect of teaching specific subject areas than to "teaching" in general.

7. The pool of potential applicants should be expanded to include high school graduates of several years past who did not go to college but who were identified as academically able by teachers and peers. [Scott found that the students graduating from high school in the spring of 1980 who did not go to college that autumn were, on the whole, equivalent academically to those who did (15)].

   The pool of potential applicants should also include housewives who want to enter the job market and midcareer adults who want job changes and may be attracted to the humanistic challenges of teaching.

   The pool of applicants should also include students who have dropped out of the university for nonacademic reasons.

8. Telephone contacts are more effective than direct mail when following up a lead. Academically able students receive far more recruitment letters than they care to read. Unless the letter is very unusual, chances are high that it will not compete with other offers.

9. Personal contact is the most effective way to attract an academically able student who has no expressed interest in teaching as a career.

10. Follow-up contacts similar to those made by football and basketball coaches are effective with students who express a slight interest in teaching but who are considering othe fields.

11. Recruitment efforts tailored to the academically able student should include quick responses to inquiries, and involve alumni in making personal follow-up calls.

RECRUITMENT EFFORTS AT ONE HISTORICALLY BLACK UNIVERSITY

Norfolk State University is the third largest historically and predominantly Black university in America. It has a rich tradition of placing teacher education high on its list of priorities.

Like most universities across the nation, Norfolk State University has initiated a number of educational reforms. Improvements have been made in recruitment, admission standards, course offerings, student advisement, student teaching and practicum experiences, instructional materials and equipment, faculty availability, school community-university collaborations, and assessment and evaluation. All of these reforms relate to the university's capability to increase the number of Black teachers prepared for the public schools. Perhaps the major recruitment effort has been the enhancement of the concept of teacher education as a university-wide responsibility.

Specific efforts have been designed to address the twin challenges of attracting a larger number of students and assisting a larger percentage of those enrolled to graduate.

The university has—

- Intiated, in 1983, the Harrison B. Wilson Honors in Teaching Program, which provides full tuition scholarships for 20 teacher education students. This program is funded through the President's nonstate funds.

- Secured a special two-year state grant of $500,000 in 1986 for scholarships, staff development, resource materials, and curriculum revisions. A follow-up grant of a smaller amount for the next two years has also been secured.

- Planned a collaborative recruitment project

with Norfolk Public Schools to work with eighth, ninth, tenth, and eleventh-grade students.

- Established a system of tutorials, workshops, seminars, and a special class to help students prepare for the NTE. (Passage rates averaged from 80 to 100 percent for the several testing dates during 1986–1987 and 1987–1988, with an average of 20 students per test.)
- Established a system of academic support for junior and senior students that includes university professors as tutors for students requiring special help in preparing for the NTE.
- Initiated, in 1980, a national annual conference on issues, problems, and strategies related to the preparation and survival of Black public school teachers.
- Enhanced the system of personal recruiting whereby professors, staff, and students (1) telephone nonreturning students, and (2) personally invite underemployed adults to telephone or visit the School of Education. Professors routinely distribute business cards to potential students.
- Initiated, in 1986, the Advanced Education Program for Paraprofessionals through which teacher aides were provided opportunities to earn teaching credentials.
- Conducted a SWITCH TO TEACHING program in 1985 to recruit military retirees, housewives, and business personnel to teacher preparation programs.
- Initiated, in 1984, an annual recruitment activity targeted at sophomores, juniors, and seniors already enrolled at the university.
- Enhanced the Two Plus Two Program, which provides a tie between the two-year community college curriculum and the university curriculum.
- Worked with the Chesapeake Public Schools to develop an Early Contract Program through which top-rated junior and senior students are recruited and offered contracts for teaching positions in Chesapeake. This tie between employment and preparation is very attractive to students.
- Initiated the Special Education Ambassadors Program, which uses alumni to recruit prospects for special education.
- Joined, in 1985, the Adopt-A-School Program in Norfolk Public Schools by adopting Ruffner Middle School. Recruitment activities in the school include sponsoring Career Day Program, Teacher Awards Night Banquet, and Citizenship Awards Program for Pupils. College students work in the school as library aides, teacher helpers, and tutors. Pupils at the school receive special invitations and tickets to participate in university athletic and cultural events.
- Initiated a program of community tutorials through which university students work with community agencies to provide academic assistance to elementary, middle, and senior high students. Agencies include the Urban League, sororities and fraternities, public housing authorities, and churches.
- Installed a special comprehensive computer-assisted curriculum laboratory through which teacher education students can upgrade their basic skills and fill in gaps they may have developed prior to college. This laboratory is also used for tutorial sessions for middle school and high school students.
- Established a Speakers Bureau through which university professors, college students, and alumni are available to speak on the need for minority teachers for community groups.

CONCLUSION

Without significant intervention, Black, Hispanic, Asian-American, and American Indian students will continue to represent a decreasing percentage of the total teacher education student pool. The teaching force in America will become more white, while the student population will become more nonwhite.

Encouraging intervention strategies have been proposed, however. Noteworthy are the efforts of historically Black colleges and universities that have devoted special resources to expand their recruitment and retention programs and to prepare students for teacher tests.

On a national level, professional organizations are gearing up to assist member institutions in recruiting and retaining Black, Hispanic, Asian-American, and American Indian students. More aggressive short-term efforts are needed to enhance the success of minority students who are enrolled in colleges and universities in general and in teacher education in paritcular. Additionally, more comprehensive long-term efforts are needed to improve the educational success for minority students throughout the educational pipeline. Further, special long-term recruitment efforts are needed. These efforts should be carefully organized, adequately funded, and effectively integrated into the total university and public school programs.

REFERENCES

1. American Association of Colleges for Teacher Education, National Commission on Excellence in Teacher Education. *A Call for Change in Teacher Education.* Washington, DC: AACTE, 1985.
2. American Association of Colleges for Teacher Education. *Minority Teacher Recruitment and Retention: A Call for Action.* Washington, DC: AACTE, 1987.
3. _____. *Teaching Teachers: Facts and Figures, 1988.* Washington, DC: AACTE, 1988.
4. American Council on Education, Office of Minority Concerns. *Minorities in Higher Education* (Sixth annual status report.) Washington, DC: ACE, 1987.
5. Association for School, College, and University Staffing. *Teacher Supply/Demand.* Madison, WI: the Association, 1984.
6. Carnegie Forum on Education and the Economy, Task Force on Teaching as a Profession. *A Nation Prepared: Teachers for the 21st Century.* New York: Carnegie Forum, 1986.
7. College Board. *Equality and Excellence: The Educational Status of Black Americans.* New York: College Entrance Examination Board, 1985.
8. Darling-Hammond, Linda. *Beyond the Commission Reports: The Coming Crisis in Teaching.* Santa Monica, CA: The Rand Corp., 1984.
9. Holmes Group. *Tomorrow's Teachers: A Report of the Holmes Group.* East Lansing, MI: Holmes Group, 1986.
10. Joiner, Burnett. In "Grambling's Efforts to Increase Test Success Rate 85 percent" by Betty Cork. *The Advertiser,* August 16, 1985.
11. National Commission on Excellence in Education. *A Nation at Risk: The Imperative for Educational Reform.* Washington, DC: U.S. Department of Education, 1983.
12. National Education Association. *Status of the American Public School Teacher,* 1985–86. Washington, DC: the Association, 1987.
13. _____. *Status of Teachers and NEA Members.* Washington, DC: the Association, 1980.
14. Pressman, H., and Gortner, A. "The New Racism in Education." *Social Policy* (Summer 1986).
15. Scott, Charlotte H. "College Desegregation: Virginia's Sad Experience." *The Virginia Quarterly Review* 58, no. 2 (Spring 1982).
16. Southern Regional Education Board. *SREB Recommendations to Improve Teacher Education.* Atlanta: the Board, 1986.
17. Whitehurst, Winston; Wiggins, Samuel; and Witty, Elaine. "Racial Equity: Teaching Excellence." *Action in Teacher Education* 8, no. 1, (1986): 52–58.
18. Witty, Elaine P. "The Impact of Educational Reforms on the Black Enrollment in Teacher Preparation Programs at Historically Black Universities." Report presented to the Virginia Department of Education. Norfolk, VA: Norfolk State University, 1984.
19. _____. *Prospects for Black Teachers: Preparation, Certification, Employment.* Washington, DC: ERIC Clearinghouse on Teacher Education, 1982.

7. THE RECRUITMENT, INCENTIVE, AND RETENTION PROGRAMS FOR MINORITY PRESERVICE TEACHERS
(Georgia Southern College)

by Livingston Alexander and John W. Miller

The recent plethora of reports, articles, and studies on the available supply of Black teachers established definitively what many had suspected for several years: there is an acute shortage of Black teachers in public school systems across the nation. Unless radical initiatives are undertaken to increase the number of Black students entering teacher education, the shortage of Black teachers will reach crisis proportions by the mid-1990s. One initiative that promises to infuse a significant number of young Black graduates into the Georgia teacher work force emphasizes collaboration among local school systems, private industry, and higher education.

This chapter (a) reviews briefly the current and projected status of Black teachers, (b) discusses the impact of the loss of Black teachers on the educational experiences of Black and white students, (c) examines the unique contributions Black teachers make to the growth and learning of Black pupils, and (d) describes an initiative to increase the number of Black teachers in Georgia. The aims of the chapter are to focus attention on the implications of having fewer Black teachers available to students and to underscore the need to take concrete, responsible action to resolve the shortage problem.

CURRENT AND PROJECTED STATUS OF BLACK TEACHERS

Several recent studies and reports define and bring into dramatic focus the problem of the shortage of Black teachers. For example, after reporting that in 1979 Blacks represented 8.6 percent of the teaching force, Garibaldi (9) cited a survey by the National Education Association for the 1985–86 school year that indicated that the numbers of Blacks in teaching had declined to 6.9 percent of the teaching force.

That there would be fewer Blacks in teaching by 1985 was not altogether surprising since, in 1980, only 3.9 percent of Black male and 5.6 percent of Black female college-bound high school seniors reported intentions to major in education (5). Projections are that Blacks will comprise less than 5 percent of the teaching force by the mid-1990s (10).

While the shortage of Black teachers is perceived as a problem that confronts public education nationally, perceptions about the severity of the problem vary in accordance with the size of the enrollment of Black students in specific regions. For example, in the southeastern United States, Black teachers comprise approximately 10 percent of the teacher work force, while Black children comprise 40 percent of the public school student population. By the 1990s, Black children will comprise 55 percent of the public school student population in Georgia. Only 6 percent of school teachers in Georgia will be Black by the 1990s (8). Those figures paint a bleak picture indeed for education in the southeastern United States generally, and in Georgia in particular.

Two compelling conclusions can be drawn from the many studies and reports that have sought to characterize the presence of Blacks in the public school teacher work force: (a) As Black teachers retire, defect from, or "test out" of the teaching profession, fewer Black graduates emerge to replace them; and (b) by the mid-1990s, Black teachers will comprise 4 percent or less of the public school teacher work force.

The dramatic reductions in the Black teacher work force from approximately 8.6 percent in 1979 to a projected 4 percent by the mid-1990s prompted one educator to estimate that "the average student, who has about 40 teachers during his precollegiate years, can expect at best to encounter only two teachers who are members of a minority group during his entire school career'' (14). If access by students to teachers of the same race is deemed important, then several crucial and sensitive questions must be asked and answered. Equally important questions, not typically confronted by policymakers, school administrators, and teacher educators, must be raised and answered about access by students to teachers of a different race, if such experiences are deemed important. The questions are: What are the consequences for Black students of limited access to Black teachers during their public school careers? And what are the consequences for white students of limited personal access to Blacks in professional roles? Does the typical white teacher possess attitudes and engage in behaviors potentially detrimental to Black students? Can Black teachers, because of their background, knowledge and functions as role models, contribute to the growth and learning of Black students in ways that other teachers cannot contribute? What viable strategies and tactics can be employed to alleviate the current and future shortages of Black teachers?

The factors that account for the persistent declines in numbers of Black teachers are numerous and complex. Extended analyses and discussions of the factors associated with the Black teacher shortage can be found in Adair (1), Garibaldi (9), and Irvine (12).

CONSEQUENCES OF LIMITED ACCESS TO BLACK TEACHERS

Numerous studies and reports underscore and document the significant role Black teachers play in the growth, development, and learning of Black students. Important features of that role involve service as positive models, surrogate parents, counselors, disciplinarians, and advocates (1, 12).

Reduced numbers of Black teachers mean that vital support structures for Black students are vanishing. Black students frequently find themselves in unfamiliar and uncomfortable settings; the support structures avert the sense of alienation and detachment Black students experience in these settings. Unfortunately, for many Black youth, the only meaningful support structures that remain exist in their peer groups.

In a commentary on her study of Black males in the environs of public schools, Grant (11) suggested that "black males seemingly enter the classroom more estranged from teachers and more tightly integrated into peer networks than most other race-gender students. For them, peer involvements strengthen resistance to school influence" (11). The estrangement and peer group dependence are very likely direct consequences of absence of meaningful involvement with significant, caring adult role models. As the potential for access to Black teachers decreases, the estrangement and peer group dependence may well intensify and characterize the experience of both male and female Black students.

Perhaps the most frequently documented asset, which dwindles in concert with the decline in numbers of Black teachers, is confidence in the ability of Black students to succeed. One purpose of a study by Beady and Hansell (3) was to determine whether the race of elementary schools teachers in predominantly Black schools was associated with teachers' expectations for future success in college and perceptions of effort. The results of the study demonstrated that Black and white teachers who taught in the schools had different expectations for the future success of their students in college. The Black teachers expected their Black students to be more successful in college than did the white teachers.

The conclusions by Beady and Hansell supported the frequently referenced study by Rubovits and Maehr (15). In their study, Rubovits and Maehr found disturbing evidence that white teachers have lower expectations for Black students than for white students. Further, the lowered expectations prompted the white teachers to give more praise, attention, and encouragement to white students than to Black students who had been described as comparably "gifted."

Findings such as those reported in Rubovits and Maehr, and Beady and Hansell surface frequently in the literature on differential effects of teacher behavior. Notable among other studies reporting similar findings about the behavior of Black and white teachers toward Black students are studies by Coates (14), Evans (7), and Simpson and Erickson (17).

In view of research findings that Black teachers tend to be more optimistic than white teachers about the achievement potential and future success of Black students, clearly, Black students are the group most adversely affected by the limited supply of Black teachers. Yet, the decline in numbers of Black teachers represents a loss for white students as well.

The importance of the role Black teachers play in the educational experience of white students is underscored in the American Council on Education report, *One-Third of a Nation* (2). The report asserts that seeing fewer Black teachers over the course of their schooling will represent a loss for white students, who otherwise only rarely are exposed personally and directly to Blacks in professional roles. Irvine (12) affirms, as well, that white students need Black teachers so that they can (a) gain a realistic sense of the multiethnic diversity in our society, and (b) modify the stereotypes and erroneous beliefs they hold about Black People. Thus, inasmuch as the schools are institutions instrumental in advancing socialization in youth, limited access to Black teachers may affect adversely the ability of white children to function productively in a culturally diverse society.

POTENTIALLY UNIQUE CONTRIBUTIONS OF BLACK TEACHERS

The most salient and frequently acknowledged contribution Black teachers make to the learning and development of Black pupils is in functioning as role models and positive examples of accomplishment and success. Yet, the potential contributions go far beyond simply serving as role models and examples. Cummins (6) identified other provisions by minority teachers that benefit minority students. The provisions include: (a) incorporation of pertinent cultural and language variations into the school program; (b) enrichment of pedagogy by using language actively to stimulate learning; and (c) blending aspects of community life into the classroom and school curriculum.

Establishing linkages between what is familiar and what is unfamiliar to Black students is a practice that comes naturally to many Black teachers. Many of the teachers are either first or second generation college graduates who retain a keen sensitivity to the needs of disadvantaged Black learners. In addition, the Black teachers maintain sufficient affiliations with the "Black community" to understand what is important and interesting to Black youth.

Another important area in which Black teachers make contributions to Black learners is in accommodating the unique cognitive and interactive styles frequently observed in Black pupils. According to Shade (16), successful functioning in the current school context requires cognitive strategies that are at variance with the strategies typically portrayed by Black learners. Shade contends that the cognitive strategies required by the schools can be described as sequential, analytical, and object-oriented, while those used by Black pupils tend to be universalistic, intuitive, and person-oriented. Peterson, Deyhle, and Watkins (13) cited research that supports the notion that accommodating differences in cognitive and interactive style is linked to higher achievement for minorities. Black teachers, who may have encountered a similar dichotomy between their own style and the cognitive strategies required by the school context in which they were educated, very likely possess the capacity to respond effectively to the learning needs and difficulties of Black youth.

It is important to note, however, that simply increasing the number of Black teachers will not assure that the unique needs of Black students will be addressed more effectively. Indeed, an analysis of requests for teacher transfers in one large urban school district revealed that the higher the percentage of Black students, the higher the number of requests for transfers by both white and Black teachers. What school districts need urgently are teachers, both Black and white, who have the will, desire, competence, and sensitivity to respond to the challenge of educating the youth of this nation.

A COLLABORATIVE PROGRAM TO REPLENISH THE SUPPLY OF BLACK TEACHERS

To address the Black teacher shortage problem in Georgia, the School of Education at Georgia Southern College has instituted a Recruitment, Incentive, and Retention Program for Minority Preservice Teachers. The objectives of the program are:

1. To cooperate with local school districts in identifying Black high school juniors and seniors who have the potential to advance into teaching careers;
2. To provide to each student financial incentives that cover all costs associated with attending college until graduation and certification; and
3. To assess the strengths and weaknesses of students and, when appropriate, provide the academic support and remediation necessary for admission into and successful completion of a program of study in teacher education.

Recruitment

In the recruitment phase of the program, local school teachers, counselors, and administrators identify promising Black high school students. Officials from the college are then invited to participate in forums involving the students, parents, school teachers, counselors, and administrators. In the forums, the college officials invite the students to consider teaching as a possible career alternative. The benefits associated with the teaching profession are explained and a pledge is made by local school officials to employ in the local community any student who completes a program of study in teacher education and qualifies for certification. To assist the students in completing their college studies, local school officials also commit financial contributions to supplement the financial aid package of each student.

Incentive

The incentive component of the program to generate Black teachers serves two important purposes. First, the incentives enable low-income students to consider the option of college attendance and possible careers as teachers. For many low-income Black students in Georgia, college is viewed as merely a remote possibility because of the exorbitant costs associated with college attendance. The second purpose served by the incentive package is that it will enable local school districts to reclaim and employ as teachers some of their most academically talented Black graduates on completion of a program of study in education.

The college develops for each student who enters the program a financial aid package that includes basic federal opportunity grants, contingent forgivable loans, scholarships, and work-study opportunities. The role of the local school districts in development of the incentive package for each student is to supplement the package with forgivable loans and scholarships that are sufficient to defray the costs associated with college attendance. A foundation program in each school district raises funds through private industry to sustain the school districts' contributions to the incentive packages. In return for their contributions to the incentive packages, school districts obtain commitments from the college students to return to the district to teach on completion of their program of study.

The commitment by the students, the responsibilities of the local school district, and the role of the college are made explicit in a letter of agreement. For example, the letter of agreement specifies that the local school district will employ the student only on the availability of a position for which the student has appropriate certification and training. The letter of agreement also specifies that a student may be required to repay grants made to the student by the school district if the student fails to comply with the terms of the agreement.

Retention

Perhaps the most important feature of the program to generate Black teachers is the retention component. Two ongoing student academic assistance programs at Georgia Southern College collaborate in assessing the academic strengths and weaknesses of students who enter the program. The programs also provide academic support to remediate diagnosed weaknesses. The support typically provided to students includes formal and informal contacts with college faculty and staff, consistent and high-quality advising, remediation in reading, math, or writing, training in study skills development, and tutoring in specific subject areas.

Although it is an important feature of the retention effort, remediation is not the focal point of the academic support provided to the students. The students who participate in the minority recruitment program typically enter with sound academic backgrounds, characterized occasionally by specific, rather than general, deficiencies. For these students, therefore, the determining factors that will assure that they successfully complete their programs of study will be the advisement system and the caring attitudes of faculty and staff. Those very practices, high-quality advisement and a caring attitude, have contributed to a retention rate at Georgia Southern that is among the highest among institutions in the University System of Georgia. Further, at Georgia Southern College the rate of retention for minority students is higher than the rate of retention for white students.

CONCLUSION

The first class of approximately 30 Black preservice teachers are matriculating currently in a program of study in teacher education. Within two years the majority of these students will assume positions as teachers in the Georgia teacher work force and, presumably, in their home communities. Two additional classes, with approximately 30 students in each class, also are now enrolled in programs of study in education. Given the cooperation and enthusiasm of the local school officials, students, and parents about the recruitment program, it is likely that many more students, who have the potential and desire to become teachers, will emerge from the local school districts.

The Recruitment, Incentive, and Retention Program for Minority Preservice Teachers is one of many initiatives striving to alleviate the shortage of Black teachers. Clearly, recruiting and training annual cohorts of 30 Black preservice teachers will not influence significantly the Black teacher shortage problem nationally or in the state of Georgia. However, when the effort at Georgia Southern College is viewed in concert with similar efforts in Wisconsin (Shorewood School District), Houston, Los Angeles, and Washington, D.C., one feels a sense of optimism that a crisis of major proportions in American education will be averted.

REFERENCES

1. Adair, A.V. *Desegregation: The Illusion of Black Progress.* Lanham, MD: University Press of America, 1984.

2. American Council on Education. *One-Third of a Nation.* Report of The Commission on Minority Participation in Education and American Life. Washington, DC: ACE, May 1988.

3. Beady, C. H., and Hansell, S. "Teacher Race and Expectations for Student Achievement." *American Educational Research Journal* 18, no. 2 (Summer 1981): 191-203.

4. Coates, B. "White Adult Behavior Toward Black and White Children." *Child Development* 43 (1972): 143-54.

5. College Board. *Equality and Excellence: The Educational Status of Black Americans.* New York: College Entrance Examination Board, 1985.

6. Cummins, Jim. "Empowering Minority Students: A Framework for Intervention." *Harvard Educational Review* 56, no. 1 (February 1986): 18-34.

7. Eaves, R. "Teacher Race, Student Race, and the Behavior Problem Checklist." *Journal of Abnormal Child Psychology* 3, no. 1 (1975): 1-9.

8. Futrell, M. H., and Robinson S. P. "Testing Teachers: An Overview of NEA's Position, Policy, and Involvement." *Journal of Negro Education* 55 (1986): 394-404.

9. Garibaldi, Antoine M. "Quality and Diversity in Schools: The Case for an Expanded Pool of Minority Teachers." Paper commissioned for the American Association of Colleges for Teacher Education's Wingspread Policy Forum, Racine, WI, 1987.

10. Goertz, M. E., and Pitcher, B. *The Impact of NTE Use by States on Teacher Selection.* Princeton, NJ: Educational Testing Service, 1985.

11. Grant, Linda. "Uneasy Alliances: Black Males, Teachers, and Peers in Desegregated Classrooms." Paper presented at the American Educational Research Association annual meeting, Chicago, 1985.

12. Irvine, Jacqueline, J. "An Analysis of the Problem of Disappearing Black Educators." *The Elementary School Journal* 88, no. 5 (May 1988): 503-13.

13. Peterson, K.D.; Deyhle, D.; and Watkins, W. "Education That Accommodates Minority Teacher Contributions." *Urban Education* 23, no. 2 (July 1988): 133-49.

14. Rodman, B. "Teaching's 'Endangered Species.'" *Education Week* (20 November 1985): 1.

15. Rubovits, C. P., and Maehr, M. "Pygmalion Black and White." *Journal of Personality and Social Psychology* 25 (1973): 210–18.

16. Shade, Barbara J. "Afro-American Cognitive Style: A Variable in School Success." *Review of Educational Research* 52, no. 2 (Summer 1982): 219–44.

17. Simpson, A. W., and Erickson, M. T. "Teacher's Verbal and Nonverbal Communication Patterns as a Function of Teacher Race, Student Gender, and Student Race." *American Educational Research Journal* 20, no. 2 (Summer 1983): 183–98.

8. A MODEL MINORITY TEACHER RECRUITMENT AND RETENTION PROGRAM: THE MINORITY TEACHER PREPARATION PROGRAM (MTP)
(University of Wisconsin–Whitewater)

by Bennett F. Berhow and Debra Knowles

Higher education remains an avenue used by minorities to improve their economic condition. Although gains have been made in providing access to higher education for ethnic minority individuals, equal educational opportunity is not yet a reality in the United States, and the underrepresentation of minorities in higher education continues to be a consequence. In fact, Hodgkinson (3) predicts a drop in the number of minority high school graduates who apply for college. For minority students who complete their secondary schooling and gain access to postsecondary education, first degree completion rates fall significantly below completion rates of white students earning their first degree (1). There is a need for innovative intervention at all levels of the educational pipeline in this country if parity in educational attainment is to be achieved by minorities in general and by Blacks, Hispanics, American Indians, and Asian-Americans in particular.

American education also appears to be moving from a surplus to a shortage of teachers (2) and guiding more talented and academically able college students into teaching and keeping them there is an effort that has gained national attention. The demand for teachers to staff the classrooms of the future will be great and the need for minority teachers will be even greater. National projections are that by the 1990s, ethnic minorities will constitute 30 percent of the school population, yet they will comprise less than 5 percent of the K-12 teaching force (1). Wisconsin projections are that by the 1990s, ethnic minorities will comprise over 15 percent of the school population (5), yet they will probably comprise less than 2 percent of the K-12 teaching force if current enrollment numbers reported by the University of Wisconsin System persist (4). Crucial to the effort to reform education is the need to staff the classrooms of the future so that they are reflective of the cultural diversity of the students constituting the elementary and secondary student population.

MTP—A PROGRAM RESPONSE TO A RECOGNIZED NEED

The Minority Teacher Preparation Program (MTP) on the University of Wisconsin–Whitewater campus was first conceived in 1985 and funded in the fall of 1986 by the University of Wisconsin System Administration. The Minority Teacher Preparation Program is the first of its kind in the University of Wisconsin System and was specifically designed to provide improved assistance and academic support to ethnic minority undergraduate students with declared majors in education. The MTP provides its service to students of Asian-American, Black, Hispanic, and American Indian backgrounds.

The University of Wisconsin–Whitewater is a comprehensive university of about 10,000 students, located in a small rural community in southeastern Wisconsin. Almost 25 percent of all degrees awarded by UW–Whitewater are in teacher education, making UW–Whitewater one of the larger teacher education programs in the state of Wisconsin. The student body comes primarily from small communities in southeastern Wisconsin and is predominantly white. Minority students who matriculate at UW–W come from urban areas that include metropolitan Milwaukee, Madison, Racine, Kenosha, Beloit, and Waukesha. The total minority student population at UW–Whitewater as recent as fall 1987 was 393 and the University of Wisconsin System (4) reported only six juniors and seniors with a declared major in education. As an institution with a small number of minority students entering teacher education and a major emphasis in teacher education, UW–Whitewater was an ideal institution to initiate a major demonstration effort in the recruitment and retention of minority students majoring in education.

The MTP is a cooperative venture that involves a partnership between the College of Education and secondary schools, two-year institutions, and campus Academic Support Programs at UW–Whitewater. "Partners in the Preparation of Minority Students for Sucess in the Teaching Profession" is a program theme that is descriptive of the programs's operating philosophy. As the first retention program of its kind in the University of Wisconsin System with an emphasis in minority teacher preparation, MTP specifically employs a model that was designed to have potential for replication at other institutions.

PROGRAM GOALS AND OBJECTIVES

Simply stated, the goals of the MTP are to attract and recruit more academically talented undergraduate minority students into teacher education and to retain, graduate, and license more talented minority students. In cultivating students for greater academic success, MTP was designed to build a supportive climate that fosters student development and expects student achievement and academic persistence. As students prepare to enter the teaching profession, they are provided with a "winning edge"—an edge gained from an elicited commitment to academic excellence and an acceptance of responsibility (as well as a sharing of responsibility) for one's success in higher education.

The specific objectives of the MTP program are—

1. To enhance minority high school and college students' awareness of career opportunities in the education profession.
2. To improve the recruitment and increase the retention and graduation rate of minority students in education.
3. To increase the involvement of enrolled students in activities designed to improve their academic performance.
4. To enhance the educational experiences of minority students through skill training and development seminars.
5. To provide opportunities for minority students to meet and exchange ideas with successful minority educators.
6. To provide academic support in the form of tutoring and counseling for students.

TARGET POPULATIONS

The students served by the MTP include students of Black, Hispanic, Asian-American, and American Indian backgrounds. On the UW–Whitewater campus, Black students represent the largest percentage of the overall ethnic minority population served, followed by Hispanic, Asian-American, and American Indian students, respectively. This pattern reflects the enrollment of minority students in public schools in Wisconsin (5) who are the focus of off-campus initiatives as MTP encourages their academic preparation for college.

ORGANIZATION

The MTP has been designed to ensure infusion of its mission and function into the ongoing operations of UW–Whitewater. The University receives funding from the University of Wisconsin System Administration to operate the MTP initiative. Although it is anticipated that external funding will not be discontinued, the reality is that this model program in minority teacher preparation receives funding through a competitive grant proposal process.

The administrative organization is summarized in the accompanying organizational chart and shows the relationships among the programs and offices at UW–Whitewater that are primarily involved in the MTP initiative (Figure 1). The chief academic officer at UW–Whitewater is the Vice Chancellor and Dean of Faculties. The College of Education Dean and the Assistant Vice Chancellor for Academic Support Services—who assumes the additional responsibility for the coordination of services to minority and disadvantaged students—report directly to the Vice Chancellor. The Assistant Chancellor for Student Affairs and Dean of Student Life is the chief student affairs officer at UW–Whitewater. The Admissions Director, Financial Aid Director, and Student Housing Director report directly to the Assistant Chancellor for Student Affairs.

Figure 1.

**UW–WHITEWATER MINORITY PREPARATION PROGRAM
ADMINISTRATIVE ORGANIZATION SUMMARY**

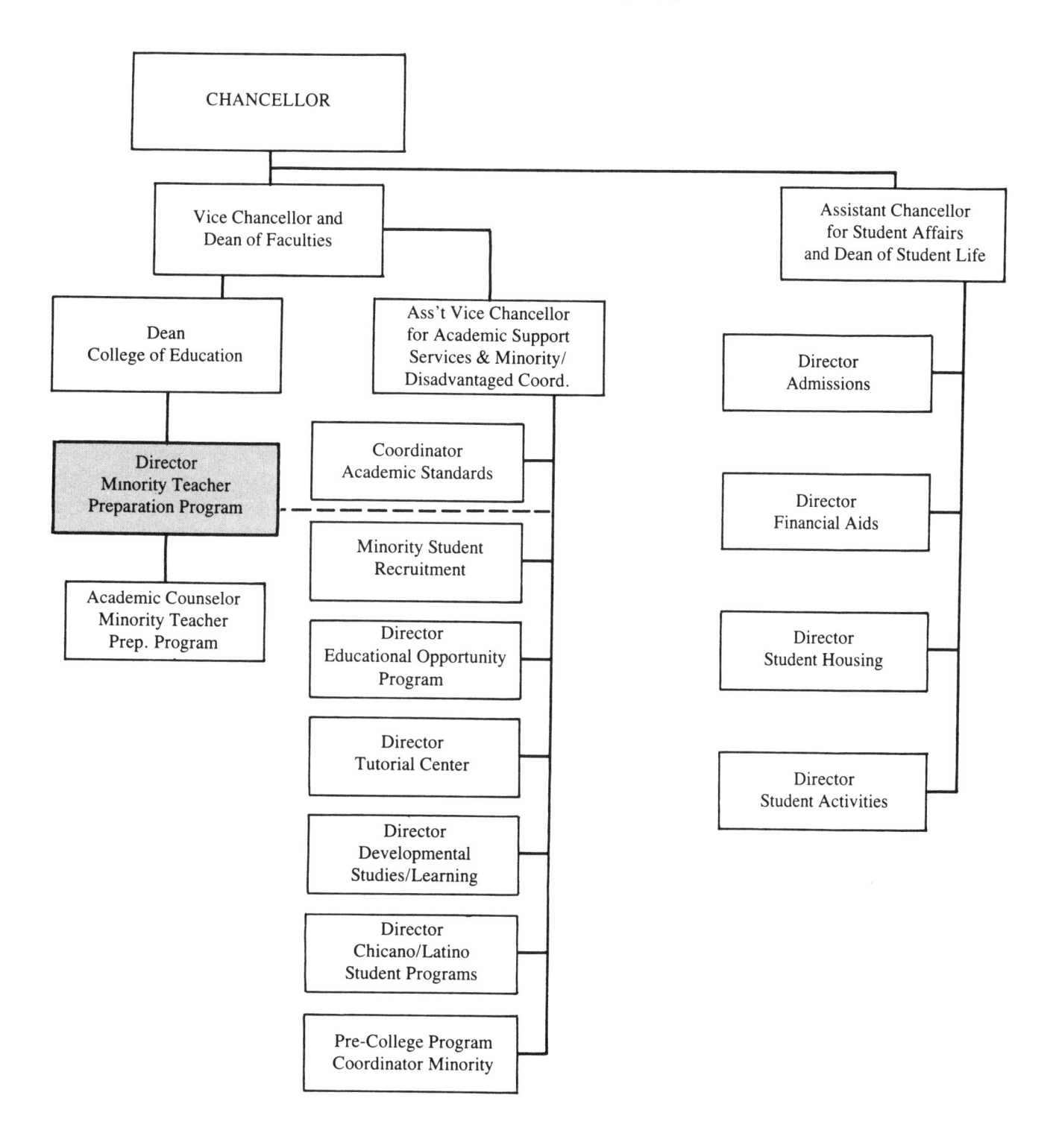

```
                            CHANCELLOR
                                │
            ┌───────────────────┴─────────────────────────┐
   Vice Chancellor and                          Assistant Chancellor
   Dean of Faculties                            for Student Affairs
            │                                   and Dean of Student Life
     ┌──────┴──────────┐                                 │
                                                         │
   Dean              Ass't Vice Chancellor          Director
   College of         for Academic Support          Admissions
   Education          Services & Minority/
     │                Disadvantaged Coord.
     │                       │
   Director             Coordinator               Director
   Minority Teacher     Academic Standards        Financial Aids
   Preparation Program
     │                 Minority Student
     │                 Recruitment
   Academic Counselor                             Director
   Minority Teacher     Director                  Student Housing
   Prep. Program        Educational Opportunity
                        Program
                                                  Director
                        Director                  Student Activities
                        Tutorial Center

                        Director
                        Developmental
                        Studies/Learning

                        Director
                        Chicano/Latino
                        Student Programs

                        Pre-College Program
                        Coordinator Minority
```

In this organizational structure, the Minority Teacher Preparation Program, which is a College of Education initiative, has a Director who reports to the Dean of the College. The Program by design works in concert with existing academic support services that are the primary component of current campus retention efforts. The MTP Director meets regularly with the academic support program managers, which include the Chicano/Latino Student Programs Director, Developmental Studies and Learning Skills Center Director, Tutorial Center Director, Educational Opportunity Program Director, Academic Standards Coordinator, Minority Pre-College Program Coordinator, and the Assistant Director of Admissions responsible for minority student recruitment. The MTP Director also meets frequently with personnel from the Offices of Financial Aid, Student Activities, and Student Housing.

The MTP Program has an academic counselor who reports to the MTP Director. The counselor meets with students on an ongoing basis and provides academic, career, personal, and social counseling. The focus of counseling is the prevention of failure through early identification and dissemination of information that strongly urges student utilization of available academic support services and faculty advisors. The MTP counselor has extensive contact with students and faculty as well as with the Offices in Academic Support Services and Student Affairs.

PROGRAM

The program has been designed to promote the academic success of students by providing tutoring and counseling and involving students in skill training, personal development, and career awareness seminars. Additionally, MTP facilitates the early identification of talented as well as at-risk students and is the link between students and the array of resources and support programs provided by the campus.

The early identification of talented minority students—students with high potential for academic success—is accomplished by cooperating with the Admissions Office and the person assigned primary responsibility for the recruitment of minority students. High school students are contacted and involved in the MTP program when they are being recruited by UW–Whitewater. This early involvement and outreach to students provides them with a greater sense that someone at the university is concerned about and recognizes their potential. This effort on the part of MTP includes involvement by current MTP participants that fosters positive peer-role modeling and increases the sense of commitment by current MTP students and potential MTP students.

The monitoring of students' academic performance and personal skill development is a continuous process. Each semester the course choices of students are reviewed and compared with their placements test scores and their past academic record to ensure that students are enrolling in courses for which they have the academic preparation. Students are also encouraged to enroll in sections taught by faculty eager to assist minority students. At the end of the semester all grades are reviewed and students are counseled and advised on actions they must take to successfully continue their pursuit of academic success and excellence. Frequently, this involves guiding students to tutorial or other support services provided for all students.

Special student seminars are scheduled that bring successful minority teachers and school administrators to the campus. These campus-based student seminars bring positive minority role models to a predominately white campus and provide students with an opportunity for interaction with these successful minority educators. Issues in education in general and in the education of minority students in particular are discussed.

Special seminars are also scheduled in public schools with large enrollments of minority students. A focus of the seminars is on the need for minority teachers and the career opportunities for minority students in the teaching profession. These seminars also involve secondary-level students and provide MTP students with another opportunity to serve as role models.

Skill development seminars focus on specific topics such as the completion of financial aids forms or scholarship applications, study skills, and writing skills. After a scholarship application seminar, for example, UW–Whitewater students received the majority of the Economic and Education Security Act

Title II scholarships awarded to minority students in the state of Wisconsin. The topics of the skill development seminars vary and are dependent on the needs of the students.

Social activities are also planned to coincide with many special seminars. As a result, students are able to interact and develop supportive relationships with other education majors and education faculty. This also helps students to discuss issues confronting teachers and to gain insight into the expectation of new teaching professionals.

RESULTS

Although the history of MTP at UW-Whitewater is a short one, two achievements are worth noting. The most important achievement is increased minority enrollment in education. When the initial program proposal was submitted for MTP in 1985-86, 33 minority students were education majors. In the first year of MTP, the number of minority students declaring education majors increased slightly to 35. In the fall 1988-89 semester, 65 minority students have declared education as their major, including 39 new freshmen and transfer students. Following the graduation of one MTP participant in December 1988, 64 minority students are enrolled in the spring 1988-89 semester. Of the 64 enrolled, 28 are juniors and seniors as compared to six juniors and seniors the University of Wisconsin System reported enrolled in the fall 1987 semester (4). Four to five graduations are expected in May 1989. Minority students are being recruited, retained, and graduated in greater numbers.

The Minority Teacher Preparation Program was also instrumental in the formulation of a Joint Cooperative Minority Teacher Training Program Agreement between the two-year Milwaukee Area Technical College and the University of Wisconsin-Whitewater. The cooperative program agreement, which was a year in the making, was signed on December 4, 1987. This agreement has been viewed as paramount in the expansion of educational opportunities for minority students enrolled at MATC and will, if successful, produce more minority teachers. More specifically, this agreement will allow minority students to earn an Associate degree at the Milwaukee Area Technical College and transfer with junior-level standing to the College of Education at UW-Whitewater. It is the first agreement of its kind in the state and clearly articulates the terms by which minority students enrolled in college parallel courses at the Milwaukee Area Technical College will matriculate to UW-Whitewater, after completion of the associate degree, to complete their training in education—earning the baccalaureate degree. There are currently over 55 minority students attending MATC who have expressed interest in becoming a teacher and the first transfer student will begin at UW-Whitewater in the fall of 1989.

The goal of MTP is to license as teachers more talented minority students. The support climate being created through a campuswide cooperative effort is working and can be replicated at other institutions of higher education. Even greater success is expected at UW-Whitewater in the immediate future.

REFERENCES

1. Baratz, J. C. *Black Participation in the Teacher Pool.* New York: Carnegie Forum on Education and the Economy, 1986.

2. Carnegie Forum on Education and the Economy, Task Force on Teaching as a Profession. *A Nation Prepared: Teachers for the 21st Century.* New York: Carnegie Forum, 1986.

3. Hodgkinson, H. L. *All One System: Demographics of Education-Kindergarten through Graduate School.* Washington, DC: Institute for Educational Leadership, 1985.

4. University of Wisconsin System. *Fall 1986 Enrollments and 1986-87 Majors by Major, Degree Level, Sex and Ethnic Group.* Madison, WI: University of Wisconsin System, 1988.

5. Wisconsin Department of Public Instruction (DPI). *Information Series No. 11.* Madison, WI: Wisconsin DPI, 1988.

9. NEW CHALLENGES FOR TEACHER PREPARATION INSTITUTIONS: RECRUITMENT AND RETENTION
(Auburn University)

by Julia L. Willard and Bruce G. Gordon

INTRODUCTION

Auburn University at Montgomery is in the process of meeting the dual challenges of recruitment and retention with innovative programs that involve faculty, staff, students, the community and the local education agencies. This [chapter] specifically addresses the Auburn University at Montgomery School of Education's efforts in recruitment, retention, and induction of education majors. These unique programs could be utilized in both private and public institutions of higher education.

BACKGROUND

Auburn University at Montgomery (AUM), established in 1969, is a comprehensive, state-funded university with undergraduate and graduate programs in education, business, liberal arts, sciences and nursing. It is located in the capital city, and between the two largest universities in the state—Auburn University, 50 miles to the east, and the University of Alabama, 100 miles to the northwest. AUM's growth in students, faculty, programs and physical facilities was rapid during the 1970s. However, in the past few years the university's growth has slowed somewhat with decreases in education majors that parallel the regional and national enrollment figures in teacher training programs. The current level of growth, university-wide, has been in the 1-4 percent range, with the enrollment staying stable in the 5,300–5,400 range.

To promote growth at AUM, Chancellor James O. Williams asked each of the five schools on campus to submit proposals designed to recruit and retain quality students. These proposals were to be unique and did not have to adhere to past guidelines or procedures. They were not to replace AUM's current recruiting efforts originating from the Admissions Office, but rather to enhance them.

All ideas and proposals submitted to the Chancellor were approved; however, some of the more extensive projects were delayed or revised because of time and/or financial restraints. A university-wide administrative retreat was held with consultants in the area of recruitment and retention. As an outcome of the retreat, the Chancellor asked each Dean to identify two faculty members who would have the specific responsibility of implementing these approved and appropriate recruitment practices beginning with the 1985-1986 academic year.

THE SCHOOL OF EDUCATION PROPOSALS

The School of Education welcomed the opportunity to present to the Chancellor innovative ideas as they related to the unique problems of education majors' recruitment and retention. Proposals and ideas ranged from tuition-free courses as bonuses to recruits and recruiters, to telephone student registration with an AUM credit card payment, and to assistance for first-year teachers during their induction year. The School of Education plans that were finally chosen for immediate implementation used a dual approach in recruitment, focusing on both undergraduate and graduate components.

UNDERGRADUATE RECRUITMENT AND RETENTION

At the undergraduate level, the AUM School of Education recruiters blitzed area high schools and junior colleges talking with students, faculty, and staff about the advantages of AUM's teacher education

---

Reprinted with permission from Julia L. Willard and Bruce G. Gordon. "New Challenges for Teacher Training Institutions: Recruitment and Retention." *Action in Teacher Education* (Winter 1987): 19–24.

programs, much in the manner of all college recruiters.

The different aspect of this recruiting was that the School of Education recruiters were offering exceptional high school students an opportunity to earn five quarter hours of credit in teacher education coursework before graduating from high school. The course, Introduction to Professional Education, was designed as an initial course for college students majoring in Education. With a few modifications for high school students, this introductory course provided instruction on the college campus and included a laboratory experiences component for the students so that they could observe and participate in actual elementary or secondary school settings. For students who might not choose education as their major, the credit could be used as an elective in a non-teaching or non-certification degree. The recruiters' main purpose in using this course was to introduce the profession of teaching to these high achievers very early in their academic career as well as to provide them with the chance to examine various career options within the field of education. It was also an opportunity for the School of Education to recruit these outstanding students much earlier than the other four competing colleges in the area.

This first offering in March 1986, was limited to high school seniors who had a minimum ACT score of 18, high school grade point average of 2.0 on a 3.0 scale, and recommendation of the high school principal or guidance counselor. The beginning class was an articulate, highly motivated group with academic credentials much higher than the required minimum. The students were conveniently registered for the course at their high schools and received a campus orientation at the initial class meeting. The local television stations interviewed these students on their first night of class, which made them feel very unique and gave the university much needed publicity for this innovative program. Their AUM instructor was an adjunct professor who was also the assistant superintendent of the local school system. This supplied some of the desired transition for these students from high school to college. All of AUM's laboratory experiences placements in Montgomery originated in this assistant superintendent's office, which enabled him to place these particular students so that they could complete their laboratory experiences for this course within easy travel time of their high schools. He also was able to match teachers with students according to learning and teaching styles since he knew both groups.

Special arrangements were made for significant university tuition reductions of more than 75 percent for these students as well as other university privileges relating to campus life, such as free library cards, free parking, and the full use of the university bookstore.

AUM is in the process of monitoring this first class of students to see if they will (1) choose AUM as their university, (2) choose education as their major, and (3) have academic success in higher education. It has already been determined by interviewing the students that their initial experiences in the schools, in higher education, and in the teaching profession have been positive ones.

As part of the junior college recruitment, and a continuation of the undergraduate recruitment, the AUM student affairs office agreed to host an annual "Program Awareness Day." This day was designed to acquaint the junior college counselors with AUM's programs, faculty, and staff. Presentations were made by top AUM administrators and recruiters describing the various programs offered by the university. The School of Education recruiters provided packets of materials for these counselors describing courses required in the teaching majors, and a step-by-step guide and schedule for assisting the junior college student in passing the very stringent state-mandated tests and other screening requirements for Admission into Professional Education.

Transcript evaluations at no cost were offered to any junior college student who wished to inquire about entering the AUM School of Education Program. These completed evaluations and program plans enabled the students to know in advance exactly what junior college courses would transfer and which ones they would need to complete during their last two years if they chose to attend AUM. This assisted the junior college counselor in advising and facilitated the transfers much more effectively, which in turn assisted in retention.

The School of Education also provided the junior college students and their counselors with a state toll-free telephone number for their use if they had questions each quarter concerning registration or equivalency course credit. This contact person was also the first person the transfer students met for orientation and advisement when they came on campus to enroll in the School of Education. The "AUM Connection" was an effective recruitment technique because the students felt very involved with AUM's education faculty and staff even as much as a year prior to their enrollment in the School of Education.

It was also decided that undergraduate recruitment within other schools at AUM was a feasible idea. Packets similar to the ones that went to the junior college counselors in the state were also sent with a cover letter to each AUM Dean and student advisor so that they could counsel students into the teaching profession if they felt it was appropriate. These students were also invited to take the introductory education course as an elective to see if teaching would be of interest to them. This recruitment had an advantage in that these students were already enrolled at AUM; therefore, they already had a commitment to the university.

The School of Education recruiters found that these students liked this introductory education course which enabled them to base their career choices on an alternative program approach based on real experiences in an elementary or secondary classroom. The School of Education held meetings with key advisors in these other schools to demonstrate that with proper selection of coursework, students could have a substantial portion of their program plan meet dual requirements in education and liberal arts or sciences.

During this period of intense recruitment for the undergraduate student, the School of Education also implemented plans for graduate recruitment. Graduate enrollment in the School of Education at AUM had decreased to the greatest extent during the previous three years. To reverse this trend a full scale effort was needed.

GRADUATE RECRUITMENT AND RETENTION

There is a large in-service teacher population in the greater Montgomery area, and the School of Education was already working very closely with the local education agencies in the placement of interns and providing laboratory experience settings for the AUM students. The school system additionally identified many of their leading teachers to serve as Cooperating Teachers for interns or student teachers. In the past it was not possible to reward these teachers for their time and expertise. One of the new recruiting practices was to identify all of these outstanding classroom teachers, who have served as Cooperating Teachers for AUM student teachers during the past few years, and offer to them a uniquely designed supervision course for graduate credit. This supervision course included components particularly helpful for them as they worked with the prospective teacher or intern. Significantly, the special tuition fee for this course for these teachers was more than a 50 percent reduction of the normal fees for five quarter hours of graduate credit. Among those teachers accepting the special course offer were both those currently in AUM's graduate program as well as those not previously enrolled in any graduate program. The threefold purpose for this recruitment technique was (1) to provide improved supervision for AUM interns through better trained Cooperating Teachers, (2) to provide a course for Cooperating Teachers that would be applicable as an elective toward completion of their graduate degree, and (3) to acquaint prospective graduate students with both the teacher education program and AUM. Just as was done with the high school students taking the special introductory education course, the status of these graduate students will be monitored to determine how many have been retained in the program.

As a result of the close association with the elementary and secondary schools in the AUM service area, the School of Education recruiters have made a ten-minute presentation to local in-service teachers during their normally scheduled weekly faculty meetings. The presentation was kept deliberately short since it was given at the end of a teaching day. These sessions spelled out specifically for each faculty member in that particular school system what either the Master's or Educational Specialist's (sixth year) degrees would mean to them from a financial standpoint. Although pay scales differ slightly between systems, the amount of time needed to pay back the expenses for tuition and books to earn a Master's degree from AUM was less than eight months with the salary increases awarded for the higher level of certification. The Educational Specialist's degree salary increase paid back tuition and book costs in approximately fourteen months. It was surprising to learn during these presentations how few teachers had ever taken the time to look at how much they would benefit financially from completing these advanced degrees or certification.

FIRST-YEAR TEACHER PROJECT

Another aspect of the graduate recruiting was the development of a course entitled The First-Year Teacher Project designed for the beginning professionals.

Acknowledging that the beginning teacher is often employed in the least desirable setting, that this teacher is frequently unsupervised and a novice in instructional motivation and management, and that the Alabama State Department of Education had no funds to implement a program for the induction process, the School of Education designed a graduate course to meet these needs. This course is offered each Fall and Winter Quarters for beginning teachers who are employed in a teaching position for the current school year. The course is designed to assist the beginning teacher in techniques of instructional motivation, classroom management, parent and administrative conferencing, and other areas of need as determined by the first-year teacher and the university supervisor. The course is offered to all beginning teachers within a hundred-mile radius of AUM regardless of the institution in which they completed their preservice education.

On-site classroom guidance and assistance are provided by the university supervisor who is a specialist in the area in which the beginning professional is teaching. For example, an elementary beginning professional would work with an AUM supervisor whose training and teaching responsibilities are in elementary education. The assigned AUM faculty member works closely with the beginning teacher in meeting assessed goals as determined by the first-year teacher and the supervisor. Observations in the classroom and relevant assignments are made by the University Supervisor, followed by conferences and individualized work sessions. The University Supervisor holds additional progress conferences with the building principal and the local education agency supervisors. These local education agency personnel are briefed frequently as a continuous process during the quarter. They are also enlisted to work as a member of the support team with the beginning teacher. Instead of the usual class sessions on campus, seminars are held so that the new professional may have the opportunity to interact with outstanding, experienced teachers and administrators who are selected from school systems other than the one in which the first-year teacher is employed. This allows the new teacher to be very open and frank about his/her feelings of concern or certain inadequacies, without the concomitant fear of evaluation procedures. These seminars are informal with much interaction among the participants. Feedback from these sessions has been very positive both from the first-year teachers and with the more experienced teachers and administrators. The principals have commented on how much more aware they are of induction problems since they have been a part of these seminars.

This innovative course, The First-Year Teacher Project, (1) combines a willingness on the part of the university to aid the beginning professional at the time when support is crucial, (2) encourages the University Supervisor to involve the local educational agency in needed reinforcements, and (3) provides the beginning teacher with the benefit of experts and additional resources at the same time of enhanced professional development and growth through graduate classes. It has also proved to be a unique way to combine induction with university recruitment and retention of quality personnel.

CONCLUSIONS

The Auburn University at Montgomery staff and faculty are committed financially and professionally to recruitment and retention of quality students. Within that framework, the School of Education emphasis for the 1986-87 academic year includes a continuation of some recruiting projects and the addition of other ideas to be implemented in the near future.

The positive feedback that has been received by the recruiters in the areas of high school, junior college, and in-service recruiting methods mandates a place in the next year's budget for the following:

1. The Introduction to Professional Education course will be offered again in Winter Quarter, 1987, to academically outstanding high school seniors. As an addition to that project, a videotape is being completed relating to the School of Education programs and includes interviews with AUM education students. These tapes will be distributed to area high schools and will be used by the counselors for students who inquire about AUM's teacher training programs. They will also supplement the usual materials originating from the Admissions Office.

2. AUM has previously courted the counselors of the area junior colleges to encourage their graduates to come to AUM. The School of Education will now invite principals and counselors from high schools in the surrounding school systems to visit the campus. They will be shown the videotape presentation of the education programs and then meet with individual faculty as well as observe AUM's prospective teachers in various course settings. This "grass roots" approach is one that will send these principals and counselors back to their schools with a realistic and positive view of AUM students and programs.

3. The First-Year Teacher Project will be offered again this Fall and Winter Quarters to school systems. Superintendents are now recommending that their new teachers enroll in the induction course and are supplying the AUM recruiters with names of first-year professionals who may be contacted by the university recruiters.

During the four academic quarters the School of Education's recruiting practices have been in effect, credit hour production at both undergraduate and graduate levels has risen to the greatest percentage in the School of Education's history. In the highly competitive market area, credit hour production at the graduate level rose 16 percent, while the undergraduate program had a 30.2 percent increase. These figures will be closely monitored during the coming academic year in view of the continuing emphasis on recruiting practices as well as new projects that are to be initiated during the 1986-87 academic year.

When the Chancellor gave each school in the university the opportunity to have a greater role in recruiting students, this challenge was one the School of Education welcomed. The faculty knew the programs and students, and the School of Education faculty were pleased to be able to promote AUM's quality programs and graduates. The first recruiting techniques have proved to be very positive during this initial year. Within the framework of financial and faculty time limitations, AUM will continue these successful recruitment, retention and induction plans, while at the same time remaining open to future plans and ideas.

10. EFFECTIVE IN-SERVICE TECHNIQUES FOR PROMOTING TEACHER RETENTION

by Ann Richardson Gayles

Educational administrators in the elementary and secondary schools of the United States who are seriously interested in improving the quality of student learning must design a systematic program for the recruitment and retention of good teachers. The central concern of this chapter focuses on identifying those specific administrative procedures and processes that will promote the retention of effective teachers. This chapter presents a philosophical discussion on how to retain high-quality teachers in the profession. The ideas are based on the author's experiences as a writer and researcher in the area of curriculum; classroom teacher on all academic levels; department head (high school, college, graduate); curriculum coordinator of a teacher education program; supervising teacher of secondary interns; and as a director of student teaching. These experiences provided an in-depth understanding of the nature of teaching—the components and conditions that either facilitate or retard its effectiveness, and the reasons why people become attracted to teaching as a profession, and why good teachers leave the profession.

The following are the basic underlying assumptions proposed:

- The teacher is the key person in a teaching-learning situation;
- The type of role the teacher plays and the quality of his/her performance depend on the philosophy of the administrators, and the nature of their administrative decisions and actions;
- One of the most promising ways for educational administrators to increase teaching effectiveness is to implement an organized program for the recruitment of talented and capable people, and for the retention of the ablest teachers; and
- A democratic educational administration is essential to quality teaching and learning.

In the democratic administrative approach, the administrator conceives of his/her primary functions as serving, not dictating to his/her co-workers; inviting and receiving suggestions and even criticisms without affront; stimulating staff to engage individually, in meaningful intellectual pursuits in terms of their recognized needs, interests, potentialities, and aspirations; and providing opportunities for teachers to work together democratically through faculty meetings, preschool workshops, in-service conferences, and on instructional committees to plan for, and implement educational programs to achieve their common goals of maximizing student learning and increasing teacher effectiveness. In this type of administration, participants will respond, communicate, and share because they are involved in the process of decision making. They will have a genuine feeling of belonging because of their closer identification with and resulting allegiance to the institution. These factors foster quality learning in any teaching-learning situation. Teacher retention is a natural result of such a teaching-learning environment (15, 19, 20, 25, 28, 36).

The great challenge and crucial educational task today is to improve the quality of learning in order to ensure the functional realization of a liberal education in a democracy. American society is committed to the task of providing its citizens with a liberal education—an education designed to improve the quality of life for the individual and society. This involves developing individuals for productive citizenship, effective service, and responsible leadership. In order to realize the aims of liberal education, teaching becomes the most compelling responsibility of society's educational institutions created for the transmission of its cultural heritage. This heritage embraces the knowledge, skills, attitudes, and values that are needed for effective personal and social development in the maintenance of a free and enriched society. This liberal education program is fundamental to the transmission and advancement of the democratic way of life, and to the development of every student toward the richest and most intelligent participation in modern society. Therefore, it is of utmost importance for educators to plan for better delivery of instructional programs and for a higher quality of learning for students through increased teaching effectiveness (12, 14, 16, 51, 52, 54, 58).

Today, effective teaching is a national concern. The accelerated interest in the improvement of the quality of learning is evident. The most central problems facing educators are in the area of classroom instruction. The effort to improve teaching is important at all academic levels; it is especially important for elementary and secondary education personnel to recognize the need for better classroom instruction and to plan for its improvement, because they provide the foundation of a liberal education. To achieve the goals of a liberal education, students must be taught effectively during the early years; they must master the developmental tasks of living in a democracy, in a sequential order, according to the principles of human growth and development (27, 38, 39, 48, 61, 67, 69).

Quality instruction has to be uppermost in the minds of educators at a time when the need for many more teachers, from whatever sources, appears imminent. The National Center for Educational Statistics (NCES) made the following observations (47): the 1980 demand for elementary and secondary teachers was 2,463,000; the projected demand for 1993 is 2,737,000; and the enrollments for elementary and secondary schools have steadily increased since 1985 and are projected to substantially increase by 1993 because of the "mini" baby boom (35, 47, 56). The increase in enrollments and the subsequent significant shortage of teachers in the near future make it imperative that educational personnel in the elementary and secondary schools begin to design a program to recruit and retain superior faculty members and to eliminate the problem of less well-trained and less experienced faculties.

The literature has revealed that the real crisis in teaching today is in who is entering the profession; too many teachers are being drawn from the bottom quarter of graduating high school and college students, and the teaching profession is attracting and retaining fewer academically able young people than it has in the past. Educational personnel must begin to do something about these alarming trends if the United States is to retain its competitive standing among world powers (32, 33, 34, 49, 59, 67, 70, 71).

This author believes that improved quality of learning is a goal that must be achieved not only by competent faculty members who have a genuine, active interest in good teaching, but also by intelligent and dedicated administrators who have a sincere interest in enhancing learning. Organized efforts by administration and faculty are essential to obtaining and maintaining superior teaching. The key to any program of instruction is the teacher. To recruit and to develop good teachers is the challenge of administrators. This requires instituting functional programs for attracting, recruiting, selecting, and retaining qualified elementary and secondary school teachers. These programs should be designed around research findings in the areas of teacher characteristics, competencies, and effectiveness, and the processes of recruitment and retention of superior teachers (7).

The administrative procedures and programs that promote the retention of superior teachers in the elementary and secondary schools of the United States are cited in the following sections.

ACADEMIC FREEDOM

Schools should give active consideration to the basic principles of academic freedom. The school atmosphere should be conducive to intellectual freedom and staff members should be encouraged to exchange ideas, information, and experiences individually and among the group. The group should be free to evaluate ideas, opinions, and data in terms of their value to the realization of cooperatively established goals. Guaranteeing freedom of opinion and expression to faculties is essential because it ensures that students also have the right to their opinions and represents the best assurance that students will be required to think. There can be no advance in knowledge unless the teacher is free to seek, to discuss, to question, and to pursue evidence (60, 64, 65).

FACULTY PARTICIPATION IN FORMULATION OF SCHOOL POLICIES

Cooperative group action for establishing school policies is essential for the existence of a good professional climate and high faculty morale. A faculty works best when it is actively encouraged to participate extensively in the planning and management of the affairs of the school and its community. Many schools appoint faculty members to serve on numerous committees. Faculty members should be given the opportunity to participate in the process of making and carrying out cooperative plans. Involvement in this kind of experience facilitates the development of communication and social skills; encourages reflective thinking, the exchange and examination of new ideas, and the making of group decisions. Participating in group planning gives each teacher a pride in the group's work, and he/she therefore does the job more effectively and loyally. Teachers who are provided with opportunities of this nature are in a position to help students acquire that knowledge and those skills needed for personal and social success in a democracy (21, 46, 60, 62).

FACULTY PARTICIPATION IN STUDENT AFFAIRS

A faculty that knows what students think and want is in a stronger position to improve instruction than a faculty that is uninformed. Therefore, administrators should encourage and provide opportunities for faculty members to serve on student committees. It is suggested that the major student organization, the student council, should and must provide for faculty participation.

If teachers are to perform their duties effectively in helping to realize the goal of education that pertains to the personal development of the individual student, they must be provided with opportunities that will enable them to understand students' needs, problems, ambitions, interests, abilities, and qualities of mind and character (31, 60, 64).

ORIENTATION PROGRAM FOR NEW TEACHERS

New teachers need to feel that they are an integral and accepted part of the school. They need (1) to understand the philosophy and objectives of the institution; (2) to become acquainted with the regulations under which the school operates; (3) to understand the various facets of the institution's curriculum; (4) to become acquainted with the resources and facilities of the school; and (5) to understand their specific responsibilities in helping to realize the objectives of the school. Therefore, it is essential that administrators design an orientation program about the general operation of the school—the functions and procedures of trustees, administration and faculty members, and the problems that inevitably arise. It is of utmost importance that the new teacher should be involved in planned experiences that will help him/her to further understand the goals of liberal learning. It is also essential that he/she receives help in the identification of resources and facilities in the school community and in the larger community that will enhance the liberal learning of students (37, 41, 42, 43, 44, 45).

FACULTY PARTICIPATION IN PROFESSIONAL ORGANIZATIONS

Teachers also must be encouraged to affiliate with and actively participate in professional and academic organizations in their respective areas. The results of such participation will lead to greater scholarship, mental vigor and alertness, improved teaching skills, as well as a greater desire to improve the quality of learning (31).

PROFESSIONAL READING ROOM

One of the characteristics of a successful teacher is scholarship. The best way of acquiring this desired trait is through a program of extensive reading of professional literature. Therefore, teachers must be provided with a wide variety of professional reading materials in a desirable and comfortable location. These reading experiences often lead to the acquisition of new and worthwhile ideas that can be used for the upgrading of teaching and the development of broad humanistic interests that will enhance the personal and social development of teacher and student.

LEAVES OF ABSENCE

Administrators should institute policies of sabbaticals and leaves of absence with full pay for study and research. Periodic leaves of absence for scholarly study and research represent one of the most potent means of increasing teaching effectiveness. A program of this kind makes it possible for teachers to make contributions to the functions of education that pertain to the advancement of knowledge.

If a system of leaves of absence is instituted, administrators should give special attention to the way in which these leaves of absence are used by teachers. Each teacher under such a program should, in conference with his/her department head, develop an outline of sequential experiences to engage in that would enable him/her to perfect his/her instructional skills or to improve those competencies that his/her position calls for at the school.

This system of leaves of absence should include incentives that will promote teacher growth through opportunities for advanced study, faculty research endeavors, exchange professorships, and educational travel (42, 50, 57, 63).

OPPORTUNITIES FOR EDUCATIONAL TRAVEL

Administrators should encourage and provide opportunities for faculty members to engage in educational travel. It is of prime importance for teachers to travel and study in foreign countries. Those faculty members with insight into other cultures, and with international experience possess a rich resource for the development of education about world affairs. Teachers who take advantage of educational travel are in a position to exercise great influence on students' ideas and attitudes about international affairs, multiculturalism, and pluralism (50, 52, 65, 66).

OPPORTUNITIES FOR ACTION RESEARCH ACTIVITIES

Administrators should also encourage and support efforts for teachers to experiment with various means of improving their teaching procedures. There must be, for example, conscious efforts to solve recognized teaching problems. Institutions of higher learning have sought to encourage and help teachers to solve those day-to-day teaching and learning problems by creating research committees that provide interest and challenge in research, and the channels of communication and the machinery needed to obtain finances, planning time, reduced teaching loads, equipment, personnel, and consultative services. Many schools have appointed a director of research and statistics to help coordinate the action research activities of their faculty.

It is through experimental investigations that education realizes its goals of advancing knowledge; obtains processes for the application of scientific data to solve some of society's problems; and utilizes effective instructional methods, techniques, and procedures that may be used to facilitate the transmission of the cultural heritage—the basic purpose of education (7, 10, 12).

INSTRUCTIONAL SUPERVISORY PROGRAM

Teachers need and want help. Therefore, an organized supervisory program should be instituted whereby teachers are given assistance with their everyday classroom problems. If a teacher is to learn how to teach better, he/she must see why improvement is important and he/she must have constant assistance. Supervision is very important in the area of instructional planning. Good planning is a key to successful teaching.

A systematic supervisory program that offers direction and counsel to faculty members should be organized by administrators and teachers, with the sole purpose of improving instruction. These programs must be faculty-centered and directed toward efforts that will enable the teacher to perform in an effective manner. Instructional supervisory programs must be organized around the specific needs and interests of teachers. Efforts should be made to encourage and motivate teachers to become involved in improvement activities (1, 2, 4).

Many schools have organized supervisory programs wherein department heads and special consultants visit classes and discuss with the instructors their strengths and weaknesses, and help them to plan for improvement. A supervisory program should also include incentives that would encourage teachers to visit one another's classes and to exchange ideas on effective teaching practices (7, 13).

PROFESSIONAL RECOGNITION OF GOOD TEACHING

Recognition of a teacher's contributions plays a major role in the decision to remain in the teaching profession. Feelings of success are important in accomplishing any goal. The teacher's quality performance depends a great deal on administrative recognition and the intrinsic reward of teaching. However, tangible rewards for outstanding teaching and ceremonies for professional recognition are great incentives for recruiting and retaining superior teachers in the profession.

IN-SERVICE EDUCATION COMMITTEE

An in-service education committee should develop assessment processes that would enable all participants to appraise the effectiveness of teaching and learning, and also institute plans to improve the quality of teaching and learning. These evaluative and improvement processes should be on a short-term as well as long-term, continual basis. The major responsibility of the committee should be to provide in-service education programs that focus on teaching as a process and as a product. It is suggested that these in-service education experiences include opportunities for teachers to seek knowledge, to express opinions, to experiment, to exchange ideas, and to obtain help on improving classroom work. In-service education should be focused on problems and means that are felt by the faculty to be vital for its development. In-service education experiences that emphasize problems that teachers say they have may be dealt with in workshops at the beginning and end of the year, through orientation programs for new teachers, teaching seminars, and periodic professional faculty meetings. These programs should always focus attention on the most productive means of upgrading instruction; and they should specifically provide for a stimulating learning environment that would enable the teacher to perform in an effective manner (3, 6, 7, 41, 42, 45, 64, 65).

PERIODIC EVALUATIONS

Periodic evaluations of teaching effectiveness by students, teachers, administrators, alumni, and self-ratings by the instructors are essential to the improvement of teaching. In fact, the process of evaluating instruction is a prerequisite to instructional improvement. Planned and continual programs of instructional evaluation should be instituted so that teachers may be given an opportunity to examine present classroom procedures more carefully in order to evaluate their effectiveness. Such processes enable teachers to distinguish more readily effective teaching practices from those which are of little value. Teachers appreciate a plan of action that will help them to improve their performances. And programs for instructional improvement promote high faculty morale, which helps in faculty retention (9).

IMPROVED WORKING CONDITIONS

In order for the teacher to perform his/her instructional tasks wisely and effectively, certain specific conditions must prevail in the workplace. The following conditions are considered to be important in providing teaching effectiveness and in promoting teacher retention:

1. *An ideal student faculty ratio.* Class size is a major factor in teacher retention. An ideal student-faculty ratio should not extend beyond a high of 25:1. Quality instruction results when classroom conditions allow for active class participation. The total maximum development of each student is possible when classroom conditions permit concern for and active attention to individual students. The educational goals of critical thinking are achieved through learning situations that provide for frequent student interchange of knowledge and ideas (1, 26, 37).

2. *Stable work assignments in terms of training, interest, and experience.* Effective teaching requires feelings of success and security. Administrators can help teachers develop these feelings by providing them with opportunities to work at tasks, for a period of time, in which they are interested, and for which they are prepared. Thus, wise administration calls for assignment of faculty members partly in terms of diversity of interests and abilities rather than solely in terms of institutional needs. Assigning

teachers to instructional and nonacademic duties in terms of their special abilities, interests, and needs will have a major impact on a teacher's decision to remain in the teaching profession (2, 6, 8, 18, 22, 26, 63, 67).

3. *Limited noninstructional services.* A teacher's workload should not be too heavy. Committee assignments, extracurricular assignments, community participation, and outside professional obligations in elementary and secondary schools should be planned and carefully scheduled on a limited basis in terms of the diversity and complexity of the multiple roles of teachers. Numerous noninstructional activities, plus the expectations of and demands by the school community and professional organizations leave little time, in many cases, for study, observation, research, and experimentation needed for quality planning, and teaching (16, 25, 30).

4. *Adequate and useful teaching facilities and equipment.* Availability of materials and equipment that will facilitate teaching and learning is an important factor in job satisfaction. Successful teaching requires the utilization of appropriate facilities and equipment. The appropriateness and adequacy of facilities and equipment is judged by their contribution to the ends sought by teachers and students. Efforts should be made to supply materials and facilities for instruction in line with the special needs and requests of teachers (2, 24, 26, 29).

5. *Adequate and competent secretarial and clerical services.* It is important for administrators to provide the various services that teachers need to carry out their instructional duties. Adequate assistance in handling routine and clerical work is of utmost importance in teaching effectiveness (23).

6. *Provision for time in the instructional schedule for personnel and guidance functions.* Understanding of a given group or of a particular individual is basic to effective teaching. Teachers learn much through personnel and guidance services that help them to gain a better understanding of students, both individually and as a group. Teachers earnestly seek to understand students as teaching methodology and content are geared toward the needs and interests of the students (4, 29).

7. *A good library.* A well-equipped library for faculty use as well as for student use plays a major role in teacher effectiveness and thereby serves as an excellent incentive for teacher retention. The availability of appropriate and adequate reading materials, audiovisual materials, and demonstration and experimentation materials is an essential condition for effective teaching and learning (10, 13).

8. *High faculty morale.* To provide the type of climate conducive to high faculty morale, efforts should be directed toward effective and impartial policies pertaining to adequate remuneration, academic promotion, sick leaves, retirement, pensions, academic freedom, tenure, workload, adequate housing, and wholesome recreation (3, 4, 5, 6, 8, 11, 17, 24, 40, 46, 55, 57).

This chapter is not intended as an exhaustive list of ways to retain effective teachers. Rather its purpose is simply to identify and suggest some of the more engaging and stimulating devices and procedures that are especially relevant to teacher retention. None of these should be regarded as panaceas. But if instituted by skillful administrators, many of the ideas may aid in narrowing the breach between what schools hope to do with students and what they actually achieve. Imaginative administrators may find some of the approaches helpful in stressing the importance and urgency of fulfilling the objectives of liberal education. These approaches may also be very useful in helping interested teachers utilize educational innovations in a productive way as they attempt to acquire further knowledge and skills in teaching that pertain to effecting open and free communication, and to developing reflective thinking.

The in-service techniques identified are concerned with administrative adjustments that facilitate quality teaching and that hopefully will promote faculty retention. These adjustments are related to conditions that would enable the teacher to perform his/her tasks in an effective manner.

SELECTED REFERENCES

1. Alexander, Lamar. "Ten Ways to Make Teaching More Attractive." *Instructor* (March 1985).
2. Ambrosie, Frank, and Haley, Paul W. "The Changing School Climate and Teacher Professionalization." *National Association of Secondary School Principals Bulletin* (January 1988).
3. Arfin, David. "Higher Entry Standards and Higher Pay May Help Ease Teacher Shortage." *Phi Delta Kappan* (March 1987).
4. Arnold, George M. "Sound Techniques, Good Fortune Ensure a First-Rate Teaching Staff." *National Association of Secondary School Principals Bulletin* (February 1988).
5. Baker, James N. "Raises, Reform and Respect; Three R's for Teaching." *Newsweek*, October 5, 1987.
6. Bennett, William J., "How Can We Improve Teachers and Teaching?" *Educational Digest* (May 1986).
7. Binko, J., and Newbert, G. "An Inservice Education Model; Teachers and Professors as Co-equals." *Journal of Teacher Education* (November/December 1984).
8. Bloch, Alfred. "The Battered Teacher." *Today's Education* (March/April 1977).
9. Borton, Terry. *Reach, Touch and Teach: Student Concerns and Process Education*. 2d. ed. Santa Monica, CA: Goodyear, 1978.
10. Boyer, Ernest J. *College and the Undergraduate Experience*. Washington, DC: American Council on Education, 1986.
11. Briggs, L. D. "High Morale Descriptors: Promoting a Professional Environment." *Clearing House* (March 1986).
12. Broudy, H. S., et al. *Democracy and Excellence in American Secondary Education*. Chicago: Rand McNally, 1984.
13. Buckley, Jerry. "A Blueprint for Better Schools." *U.S. News and World Report*, January 10, 1988.
14. Carnegie Forum on Education and the Economy, Task Force on Teaching as a Profession. *A Nation Prepared: Teachers for the 21st Century*. New York: Carnegie Forum, 1986.
15. Chickering, Arthur W., et al. *The Modern American College*. San Francisco: Jossey-Bass, 1981.
16. Coates, Thomas, and Thoresen, Carl. "Teacher Anxiety: A Review with Recommendations." *Review of Educational Research* (Spring 1976).
17. Cook, Donald. "Teacher Morale: Symptoms, Diagnosis, and Prescription." *Clearing House* (April 1979).
18. Council for Basic Education. *Making Do in the Classroom: A Report on the Misassignment of Teachers*. Washington, DC: Council for Basic Education, 1985.
19. Cremin, Lawrence. *American Education*. New York: Harper & Row, 1981.
20. _____. *Public Education*. John Dewey Society Lecture, No. 15. New York: Basic Books, 1976.
21. Duttweiler, Patrick C. "Organizational Changes to Attract and Retain Qualified Teachers." *Clearing House* (April 1987).
22. Edgerton, Susan K. "Teachers in Role Conflict: The Hidden Dilemma." *Phi Delta Kappan* (October 1977).
23. Educational Research Services, Inc. *Fringe Benefits for Teachers in Public Schools*. Washington, DC: Educational Research Services, 1985.
24. Engel, Ross A. "Creating and Maintaining Staff Morale: Personnel Administrator's Role in a Time of Ferment in Education." *Clearing House* (November 1985).
25. Feistritzer, C. E. *The American Teacher*. Washington, DC: Feistritzer Publications, 1983.
26. Finn, Chester, E. "Nine Commandments for School Effectiveness." *Education Digest* (January 1985).
27. Ford, Jerry D. "The Decline of Confidence in Leadership." *Clearing House* (January 1987).
28. Frady, Marshall. *To Save Our Schools, To Save Our Children*. Far Hills, NJ: New Horizon Press, 1986.
29. Fuller, F. F. "Concerns of Teachers: A Developmental Conceptualization. *American Educational Research Journal* (April 1979).
30. Gaede, Owen F. "Reality Shock: A Problem Among First-Year Teachers." *Clearing House* (May 1978).
31. Geronimo, Joe Di. "Boredom: The Hidden Factor Affecting Teacher Exodus." *Clearing House* (April 1987).
32. Good, Thomas L., et al. *Teachers Make a Difference*. New York: Holt, Rinehart & Winston, 1975.
33. Goodlad, J. I. *A Place Called School: Prospects for the Future*. New York: McGraw-Hill, 1983.
34. Graham, Patricia A. "Black Teachers: A Drastically Scarce Resource." *Phi Delta Kappan* (April 1987).
35. Graybeal, William S. *Teacher Supply and Demand in Public Schools*. Washington, DC: National Education Association, 1981.
36. Grubb, W. Norton, et al. *Broken Promises: How Americans Fail Their Children*. New York: Basic Books, 1982.
37. Hendrickson, Barbara. "Teacher Burnout: How to Recognize It, What to Do About It." *Learning Journal* (1979).

38. Housam, Robert B., et al. *Educating a Profession*. Washington, DC: American Association of Colleges for Teacher Education, 1976.
39. Jennings, Lane, and Cornish, Sally, eds. *Education and the Future*. Washington, DC: World Future Society, 1980.
40. Knoblock, Peter, and Goldstein, Arnold P. *The Lonely Teachers*. Boston: Allyn & Bacon, 1971.
41. Kreis, Kathleen, and Milstein, Mike. "Satisfying Teachers' Needs: It's Time to Get Out of the Hierarchical Needs Satisfaction Trap." *Clearing House* (October 1985).
42. Lambert, Linda. "Staff Development Redesigned." *Phi Delta Kappan* (May 1988).
43. Landsmann, Leanna. "Warning to Principals: You May Be Hazardous to Your Teachers' Health." *National Elementary School Principal* (March 1979).
44. Lembo, T. *Why Teachers Fail*. Columbus, OH: Charles E. Merrill, 1971.
45. Lieberman, L., and Miller, Lynn. *Teachers, Their World, and Their Work: Implications for School Development*. Alexandria, VA: Association for Supervision and Curriculum Development, 1984.
46. Nagi, Mostafab, and Pugh, Meredith D. "Status, Inconsistency, and Professional Militancy in the Teaching Profession." *Education in Urban Society* (August 1973).
47. National Center for Educational Statistics. *Conditions of Education*. Washington, DC: U.S. Government Printing Office, 1985.
48. National Commission on Excellence in Education. *A Nation at Risk: The Imperative for Educational Reform*. Washington, DC: U.S. Department of Education, 1983.
49. National Education Association. *The Status of the American School Teacher*. Washington, DC: the Association, 1982.
50. Orlander, H. T., and Farrell, M. E. "Professional Problems of Elementary Teachers." *Journal of Teacher Education* (April 1970).
51. Ravitch, Diane. *The Schools We Deserve: Reflections on the Educational Crisis of Our Times*. New York: Basic Books, 1985.
52. Raywid, Mary A., et al. *Pride and Promise: Schools of Excellence for All People*. Westbury, NY: American Educational Studies Association, 1985.
53. Reed, Sally. "What You Can Do to Prevent Teacher Burnout." *National Elementary Principal* (March 1979).
54. Rodgers, Frederick A. "Past and Future of Teaching: You've Come a Long Way." *Educational Leadership* (January 1976).
55. Rosen, Sherwin. "Some Economics of Teaching." *Journal of Labor Economics* (October 1987).
56. Roth, Robert A. "Teacher Supply and Demand Studies: Future Trends." *The Education Digest* (May 1982).
57. Russell, Daniel W., et al. "Job-Related Stress, Social Support, and Burnout among Classroom Teachers." *Journal of Applied Psychology* (May 1987).
58. Sarason, Seymour. *Schooling in America: Scapegoat and Salvation*. New York: Free Press, 1983.
59. Schlechty, P., and Vance, V. "Recruitment, Selection and Retention: The Shape of the Teaching Force." *The Elementary School Journal* (April 1983).
60. Schimmel, David. "To Speak Out Freely: Do Teachers Have the Right?" *Phi Delta Kappan* (December 1972).
61. Scott, Peter. *The Crisis of the University*. Dover, NH: Longwood, 1984.
62. Sickler, Joan L. "Teachers in Charge: Empowering the Professionals." *Phi Delta Kappan* (January 1988).
63. Sparks, Dennis. "Teacher Burnout: A Teacher Center Tackles the Issues." *Today's Education* (November/December 1979).
64. Stinnett, T. M., ed. *The Teacher Drop-Out*. Itasca, IL: F. E. Peacock, 1970.
65. Stinnett, T. M., et al. *Professional Problems of Teachers*, 2d ed. New York: Macmillan, 1963.
66. Sullivan, Patricia, and Salisbury, Susan. "Teacher Burnout: Why the Best Are Quitting." *Fort Lauderdale News/Sun Sentinel,* March 30, 1980, 1A, 10A.
67. The Holmes Group. *Tomorrow's Teachers: A Report of the Holmes Group*. East Lansing, MI: Holmes Group, 1986.
68. Victor, S. Vance, et al. "The Distribution of Academic Ability in the Teaching Force: Policy Implications." *Phi Delta Kappan* (September 1982).
69. Welsh, Patrick. "Teachers Fight for Their Own Profession." *Education Digest* (September 1987).
70. Wise, Arthur E. "Selecting Teachers: The Best, the Known, and the Persistent." *Educational Leadership* (February 1988).
71. Wise, Arthur, et al. "Effective Teacher Selection." *Educational Digest* (November 1987).
72. Woodring, P. "The Persistent Problems of Education." *Phi Delta Kappan* (1983).

11. DEVELOPING THOUGHTFUL PRACTITIONERS: A SCHOOL/UNIVERSITY COLLABORATION FOR RETAINING FIRST-YEAR TEACHERS

by Mary Gendernalik Cooper and Ann I. Morey

The New Teacher Retention Project is a collaborative partnership between San Diego State University and the San Diego Unified School District. The purposes of the Retention Project are to develop a practical model of support and assistance to new teachers, particularly those working with students from culturally diverse backgrounds, and to promote the retention of these teachers in such settings. The Retention Project involves university faculty from the arts and sciences (as well as faculty from the College of Education), along with staff development personnel, resource teachers, mentor teachers, and administrators from the school district. The project is jointly administered by the university and the school district. The Dean of the College of Education serves as the project's principal investigator and primary liaison to the President of San Diego State University, the Chancellor's Office of the California State University system, and the Superintendent's Office of the California Department of Education. Two co-directors and an executive director share administrative responsibilities. The university-based co-director is a senior faculty member whose scholarship and expertise are in the areas of child development and educational programs and practices that are learner-centered; the school district-based co-director is the director of the staff development department in the school district. Her responsibilities include all professional growth and development initiatives within the school district. The executive director is responsible for the general management of the project, university-based personnel assignments, coordinating program component development, implementation and evaluation, budget development and monitoring, and internal documentation and evaluation. Collectively these four individuals provide the project's policy leadership.

The Retention Project is supported by a four-year grant, which is jointly funded by the Chancellor's Office of the California State University system and the Superintendent's Office of the California Department of Education, as well as by contributions of the two collaborating institutions.

This chapter discusses the three major assistance components of the project: professional development, psychological and collegial support, and scholarships and materials stipends. The process of collaboration employed in the project and insights gained through it are also discussed.

PROFESSIONAL DEVELOPMENT COMPONENT

The professional development component of the Retention Project reflects a number of beliefs, shared by the project developers, about both teaching and the types of assistance new teachers need. First, teaching is conceptualized as a highly complex integration of knowledge and understanding, strategic and technical skills, attitudes and dispositions, analytic and synthesizing capabilities. Second, judgments teachers make in practice are pivotal influences on student learning, and the soundness of these judgments is a function of the depth and richness of these domains. Sound judgment can only be developed within the context of actual practice, but not without shared reflection, assistance, and collegial support. The environment of practice, therefore, must both encourage and value that development. This conception of teaching differs significantly from the narrowly technical and implicitly condescending "teacher-proof" notions embedded in the generic teaching effectiveness prescriptions that have been so pervasive in recent years.

Three key implications for structuring systematic assistance to new teachers follow from this conception. First, recognizing that the new teacher's first teaching assignment constitutes a period of transition, any assistance must address both continued acculturation to the profession (i.e., development of sound judgment, thoughtful informed practice, and a professional self-image defined in terms of these qualities) and acclimatization to the school and school district. Second, the assistance must be structured in such a way that it simultaneously reveals the knowledge and skills the new teacher brings to the enterprise and helps the new teacher contextualize the application and adaptation of that knowledge and those skills to his/her actual situation. Third, the assistance must encourage the new teacher's confidence in her/his ability to work through problem situations and to engage with colleagues in shared problem solving.

In addition to responding to these implications, the project developers have structured this component of the Retention Project to minimize communicating a "survival" mentality to the new teachers, which too often translates to quick fixes for controlling and manipulating students. This concern takes on added poignancy when new teachers are working with culturally diverse populations. Finally, they have been cautious in structuring the content of the project on the basis of the new teachers' perceptions of what they need. Their inexperience can lead them to confuse symptoms with problems, and to the unrealistic expectation that prepackaged, universally applicable answers exist. Projects that are solely "response"-structured can easily fall prey to "doing for" or "doing to" teachers, without actively engaging the new teachers' judgment or intellect. They engender both a sense of dependence and disillusionment. The latter eventuates when, believing there are "answers," teachers are told what to do, they do it (most often without any thought to context variables that might indicate adaptation rather then direct application), it does not work, and they feel cheated.

Over the course of the three years, the Retention Project has developed the following structures, procedures, and content for the professional development component of the project. New teachers participating in the project are grouped by their schedules (San Diego Unified School District actually runs five different schedules, with four tracks of year-round school and a traditional ten-month schedule), and by grade clusters if possible (primary, intermediate, middle school). Each group consists of no more than six new teachers (a faculty member from the College of Education at the university leads each of these clusters). Cluster leaders are selected on the basis of their expressed interest in working with new teachers and school district personnel as well as their subject matter/pedagogical expertise. This expertise results in a strong interdisciplinary team.

A number of factors were considered in establishing cluster size. First, the clusters needed to be small enough that the new teachers and their cluster leader would be able to establish a group identity, get to know each other, and have sufficient opportunity to actively participate in cluster meetings. The cluster size would also accommodate meetings between or among clusters without such situations becoming unwieldy. This cluster size translated easily into instructional load credit or units for the faculty members. Under the college's supervision formula, this ratio equals three units, which is also the standard number of units for a single course. This arrangement has the additional advantages of accommodating to changes in the number of new teachers and of establishing a standard cost measure for faculty services.

Each of the new teachers is also assigned a mentor. These expert teachers from the school district are matched with the new teachers on the basis of similarity in grade, curriculum, and student assignments. Throughout the year the mentors work with their partnered new teacher individually and in the clusters.

The professional development component of the Retention Project is organized into a year-long series of evening seminars, release-day workshops, and classroom visits. The content of the seminars and release days include issues and strategies related to each of the subject areas in the curriculum, understanding and working with youngsters from diverse backgrounds, classroom management and discipline, working with other adults in the school setting (particularly parents and teacher aides), and personal stress management. The strategies used to address these content areas consistently reflect the overall project purposes of acculturation and acclimatization. Seminar sessions are three hours long and occur each week that a cluster is in school, unless a release day has been scheduled. Over the course of the school year, the new teachers participate in a total of ninety hours of combined release days and seminar time. In general, seminars consist of three segments. One segment includes a presentation on a specific content topic followed by discussion through which the new teachers interact with the presenters on relating the presentation to their own teaching situation (for this part of the seminar, a number of clusters may be together). Another segment consists of time for critical incident writing, during which each new teacher writes about something important to her/him that has occurred in their class or school. The third segment is a cluster discussion during which the new teachers may share their critical incident and seek input on strategies or related experiences others may have had, or during which there is further discussion of the earlier presentation.

The presentations are jointly planned by the school district and university personnel and, when possible, jointly presented. The presentations always include information about resources (people, materials, places) available through the school district, university, or broader community, and suggestions regarding how to access them. Issues of adaptation and contextual appropriateness are always included in the discussions following the presentations. This is accomplished through a number of strategies. A new teacher may ask how something presented would be adapted to a multiple language class, or how it might be employed with a particular text series or curriculum. It also might be accomplished through the presenter posing questions about application, appropriateness, adaptation, and possible problems to the new teachers. The purpose is to address issues and questions of practice thoughtfully.

The critical incident writing is also employed to promote thoughtfulness about practice. It affords the new teachers an opportunity to reflect on what they and their class are doing, why things are happening as they are, what they are pleased with and want to sustain as well as what they think they need to change. The critical incidents reported by the new teachers are not necessarily problems or negative events. The new teachers have written about progress they have made in an area of concern, events that have boosted their self-confidence, or flashes of insight that writing helps them preserve. For example, one new teacher came to the realization that organizing materials and establishing routines with her first-graders actually enhanced her ability to implement a child-centered philosophy. Another teacher explained in a series of essays how the reinforcement-based management plan she was using was generating appropriate behaviors (when the teacher was watching) in students, but was not engendering the types of attitudes she wanted to foster in the children. She has used the writing opportunities to explore, explain, and evaluate alternatives that will address this goal.

The new teachers are not required to discuss what they have written with their clustermates. They do, however, turn them in to their cluster leader for written response or comment. This provides a systematic means of confidential communication and affords the cluster leader a regular opportunity to interact with each new teacher. Cluster leaders also report that the critical incident writing alerts them to the need for individual assistance and to instances of confusing symptoms with problems.

The cluster discussion portion of the seminar can take a number of directions, depending on the needs and interests of the group. Much of the time in these sessions is utilized in sharing experiences, commiserating, problem sharing and problem solving. They provide the new teachers with an opportunity to practice being collectively thoughtful, albeit highly practical, about teaching.

The release days (5 throughout the year) usually focus on a topic fairly new to the teachers and therefore requiring a longer concentration of time. Familiarizing the new teachers with the school district curriculum, related materials and resources, for example, was the topic of an early release day. During this workshop, the new teachers had an opportunity to go through the various subjects with content specialists from the school district to explore points of emphasis, areas that might be problematic, and variations that could be employed within the given framework. Another release day is scheduled to help the new teachers become familiar with and comfortable using cooperative learning strategies. Here the release day affords the opportunity to try some things out in the safe and helpful company of colleagues. Mentor teachers often participate in the release days with the new teachers, frequently as presenters or demonstrators.

Through participation in the seminars and release days, the new teachers also have the opportunity to earn six units of graduate credit from the university or the same number of continuing education units from the school district. The accumulated hours can be counted toward the state's requirement of 150 hours of continuing education every five years.

One of the more perplexing and persistent problems involves the determination of appropriate course expectations for earning credits. Traditional reading and writing assignments are often perceived by the new teachers as added burdens. The problem was solved by requiring that the new teachers prepare two case reports on issues they choose and which may be elaborations of a critical incident. The case reports include a reflection/analysis component as well as the description of an event or situation.

Project funding is used to pay for the substitute teachers on release days, any outside consultants, after-work hours for district resource teachers and mentors, and university fees for the graduate credits.

PSYCHOLOGICAL AND COLLEGIAL SUPPORT

This component of the Retention Project is designed to minimize the sense of isolation and abandonment so many new teachers report having experienced in their first years of practice. The central feature of this component is the assignment of the new teacher to an expert mentor teacher as soon as possible after the new teacher has been hired. The mentor teachers, who are selected through a formal process in the district and receive specific training related to the mentoring role through the staff development department, are pivotal to successfully acculturating and acclimating the new teachers. Through meetings with project administrators, they come to understand and contribute to the conception of teaching described at the beginning of this chapter. To the new teachers, the mentor teachers personify credibility. They represent successful practice, ability, virtuosity in what the new teacher is about to try. They possess the knowledge of the district as a distinct culture; they know how it works. They demonstrate the seasoned and balanced perspective that encourages risk-taking and engenders stability. New teachers consistently report the invaluable resource their mentors have been.

In addition to the mentor teachers, the cluster structure also helps the new teachers establish connections with their peers. The cluster leader prevents the new teacher from feeling isolated from the university.

The staff development office of the school district assigns one of its resource teachers to the Retention Project. This is a half-time assignment, supported by project resources. This person serves as a critical liaison between the new teachers and the various administrative and resource departments of the school district. This resource teacher also fills a key planning and logistics role in the development of all facets of the project.

The support strategies are less formally structured than those in the professional growth component. The project provides resources for the new teachers to visit and work with their mentors and to have the mentors observe and consult in their classes. None of the project support personnel participate in any way in the performance evaluation of the new teachers. This has been a source of reassurance to the new teachers, encouraging them to be candid and open. Project personnel do, when the situation warrants, advise and counsel the new teachers regarding their professional impressions of the advisability of the new teacher continuing in the education profession. These eventualities are seen as professional responsibilities and are handled with utmost confidentiality.

One of the clearest indicators that this approach to collegial support is helpful comes from the new teachers, their building colleagues, and principals, all of whom report that participation in the project promotes a sense of confidence about working with colleagues and asking others besides those in the project for help, information, and advice.

SCHOLARSHIP AND MATERIALS STIPENDS

The third assistance component of the Retention Project provides scholarship stipends to the new teachers for the university fees related to the graduate units. It also provides each new teacher with a $300 instructional materials stipend. This stipend makes it possible for the new teachers to acquire materials not provided by the school district. The availability of the stipend has encouraged the new teachers to become more critical consumers, considering long-term or diversified uses of potential purchases. It has prompted them to explore very carefully which resources and materials the district will provide them with so that their own purchases do not turn out to be duplications. It has also been a practical prompt for them to seek the advice and assistance of their mentors, cluster leaders, and other resource personnel. The stipend has made purchase of materials another dimension of thoughtful practice. The new teachers gain access to the stipend by completing a request form that includes a rationale for the purchase. The new teacher's mentor, cluster leader, and the staff development resource teacher review the requests prior to disbursement. Frequently, the new teachers consult with these individuals about intended purchases and in so doing can ascertain if it is a wise purchase. The new teachers are limited to using no more than half of the stipend before January. Prior experience illustrates that this simply helps the new teachers give more critical thought to the investments they eventually make. The materials purchased with the stipends belong to the teachers, a tangible reminder of participation in the program.

COLLABORATION

School/university collaborations, as the literature suggests, are largely symbiotic in nature and synergistic in process. To be productive and resilient, collaborative efforts require that the institutions involved clearly recognize their essential differences in goals, priorities, modes of operating, organizational dynamics, language and culture. Collaboration, if it is to be fruitful, also depends on the participating institutions resisting inclinations to co-opt each other. The strength of any collaboration lies in the sustained independence, distinct expertise, resources, and perspectives each brings to the partnership. This is not to say, however, that within the actual workings of the partnerships, people's ideas, perspectives, and positions are not altered. Collaboration is a powerful vehicle for understanding, which in turn contributes to shared and creative problem solving as well as risk-taking initiatives that eventuate in mutual benefit.

Synergy denotes actions of two discrete agencies, which when undertaken in concert with one another, produce a total effect that is greater than the sum of the two effects generated independently. Successful collaboration is marked by this process. In the Retention Project, the time and energy invested in joint planning, implementation, review and revision has inevitably produced a finer quality program than would be possible through wholly separate efforts or even through cooperation.

A critical distinction between collaboration and cooperation is worth noting here. In the former, there is a shared purpose and agenda emanating from an issue or situation in which each partner feels a compelling interest. It may relate to only a single area of each partner's total domain of responsibility; each may be concerned with a distinct facet of it, but both institutions have some commitment to or interest in addressing it. Cooperation does not necessarily involve such a shared concern. It often can be accomplished with far less resource investment than can collaboration.

In the Retention Project, the shared purpose relates to the continued professional development and quality of practice of new teachers. Both partners bring resources and expertise to bear on the acculturation domain of this goal. Both can contribute substantially and in complementary ways to the acclimatization process as well. The collaboration of personnel from both institutions on this shared purpose generates a richer, more comprehensive product than either could generate separately.

A number of actions and conditions have contributed significantly to the Retention Project both in terms of its surviving and in terms of success in realizing its purposes. These conditions are pertinent to any interinstitutional partnership. A summary of these conditions follows.

- The chief executive/administrative officers of each institution must affirm and periodically reaffirm institutional commitment to the collaboration.

- Personnel from each institution who share responsibility for policy and administrative leadership of the collaboration must have sufficient positional authority and access to policy making/influencing within their own institution to be able to effect partnership work.

- Sufficient resources must be available for both the administrative/policy work of the partnership and implementation of collaborative initiatives. Two explanatory points are important here. Involvement in collaboration, especially in its initial stages, requires foundation laying—regular sustained discourse. Without resources to make that discourse possible within an individual's work assignments, resentments and disinterest are easily fostered. Collaborative initiatives take place, for the most part, as pilots within a "business as usual" environment. The surrounding programs and responsibilities of each institution are not suspended. Distinct resource availability to the collaboration is prudent and can reduce the likelihood of sabotage and discord between the collaboration initiatives and traditional programs and procedures.

- Broad-ranging involvement of personnel from diverse sectors of the institutions and a regular flow of information/communication regarding the collaboration serve to extend interest and commitment. They also increase the opportunity for richer, more creative collaborative work by encouraging varied ideas and perspectives.

- As important as administrative involvement is, investment of the largest portion of resources committed to the collaboration should be directed to actual initiatives and to those implementing the initiatives. The proper balance is, of course, situation specific.

- As much as possible, it is important to minimize the creation of separate policy and project review structures. Pertinent structures that already exist within each institution should be kept apprised of the collaborative work and build the needed support networks through them. This strategy can contribute substantially to institutionalizing both collaborative processes and the programs such work produces.

- Do not ever lose sight of or minimize the importance of open honest communication among partners; issue-based arguments or strongly stated perspectives about issues often serve as conduits for understanding and creativity. Take breaks, but always come back! One of the truest indicators of a working collaboration is when individuals from different institutions align on an issue and together take on their colleagues.

- Collaboration requires patience, perserverance, risk-taking and enthusiasm. Maintaining these, among all involved, frequently falls to the individual responsible for daily administrative direction of the collaboration. But everyone has to be alert to signals that communicate needed encouragement or reassurance. Keeping folks talking, exploring, and pursuing the shared purpose in a good-natured way is a critically important task. Informal conversations or get-togethers can facilitate this. Good-natured teasing, joking, and humor (even banter) in formal meetings are invaluable. Informal follow-up with individuals also serves to solidify candor and continued communication.

- Institutional leaders not directly involved in the day-to-day operation of the collaboration need to be kept informed of proceedings, issues, dilemmas, and so forth. In addition to being a basic professional courtesy, it can be of very practical value. it will promote the continued support of these critically important individuals; it protects them and the endeavor from being blindsided; it provides another perspective. These individuals can provide useful insights about strategies and tactics that will benefit the collaborative work. The process can be mutually satisfying.

- Clerical support specifically assigned to the collaboration is crucial. The logistics of this mode of operating are far more cumbersome than any other process. These resources contribute to the partnership's stability, efficiency, and ultimately, efficacy.

- Finally, self-regulated restraint on the part of all involved parties is absolutely essential. For the most part, key players in the collaboration are "movers and shakers" in their own institutions. They need to recognize the need for and contribute· to the collaboration establishing its own foundations of understanding and mutual respect. They also need to understand that for the collaboration to be effective, it needs to transcend traditional institutional boundaries.

Since, at its core, collaboration entails creative problem solving and synergistic action, it requires considerable autonomy from standard operating procedures. Knowing how and where to leverage or manipulate those procedures as well as when not to veer too far afield is what makes the involvement of those individuals with the positional authority mentioned above so critical. These individuals also bring understanding of their institution's pervasive and sometimes intractable contextual realities. These realities necessitate restraint on the part of external sources of support to the collaboration. Failure to recognize contextual conditions or constraints and to incorporate those considerations in the form or shape of collaborative initiatives will minimize, if not obviate, the initiatives' intended effect. Noting such conditions often accommodates eventual exploration of the intractables, their merit and utility to the institution, and possibilities for reshaping them. Such entries are foreclosed when collaborative work is externally mandated.

INSIGHTS

The Retention Project provided assistance and support services to twenty-five new elementary teachers in each of the first two years. In this third year, thirty-six new teachers are participating in the project. Considerable insight and practical understanding has been accumulated about new teachers as emerging practitioners, and about strategies that can promote a thoughtful dimension in that process. These are briefly summarized here.

New teachers quickly, but with no small amount of surprise, come to recognize that teaching is psychologically, intellectually, and physically arduous. Their surprise at this is just one of a number of perplexing perceptions that they bring to teaching. Another is that they believe they ought to know, in the sense of already being accomplished at, how to do things that they have never done before. And third, they tenaciously persist in believing that there are "answers" out there that they can simply superimpose on their own classes and that will transform them to some ideal condition. These beliefs and perceptions reflect a not yet fully developed conception of the inherent complexities of teaching.

Many of the new teachers also demonstrate an understandable preoccupation with the immediate and practical. Their attention and energies are exclusively focused on the proximate. They often demonstrate limited confidence in their own ability to apply or utilize what they have learned and do know. Rather than viewing these traits as maladies or deficiencies, which can engender a "doing to" or "doing for" response, they are viewed as simply the conditions with which to start. These traits are both natural and understandable. Indeed they are the reason neophytes need structured support and assistance to advance their professional development.

Assistance then is multifaceted. It must include personal reinforcement along with encouraging personal initiative, self- and peer reliance. It has to be structured to simultaneously foster self-confidence and commitment to continuing to build a sound basis of knowledge and skill to sustain that confidence. Most importantly, it has to emanate from the reality of their teaching, from the problems, situations, conditions, and content of their own work.

The structuring of the support network, coupled with thoughtful reflection on their own experiences, promotes attending to the immediate while simultaneously developing habits of mind and practice that will sustain these teachers well beyond the first year.

APPENDIXES

A. OVERVIEW OF ETHNIC MINORITY GROUPS FROM NEA's... *AND JUSTICE FOR ALL*

American Indian/Alaska Native

From the first attempts at educating American Indians, the goal has been to change them. The Jesuits attempted change by acquainting the Indian with the French manner, French customs, and French language. The Protestants tried to Anglicize Indians and prepare them for a "civilized" life. The Franciscans worked to bring Indians into the mainstream by making them missionaries. Schools were established as further attempts at "civilizing and converting" the natives.

Every attempt at changing the American Indian and, now, the Alaska Native has met with failure or minimal success. Early approaches at changing the American Indian are explained in an 1899 statement by a top government Indian affairs official:

> "The settled policy of the government is to break up the reservations, destroy tribal relations, settle Indians upon their own homesteads, incorporate them into the national life, and deal with them not as nations and tribes or bands, but as individual citizens. The American Indian is to become the Indian American...."

As this statement makes clear, Indian education policies have historically had two thrusts: isolation and assimilation. Both these thrusts have been challenged by Indian people: "Indians today are deeply concerned with getting effective and relevant education for their children. They want the educational system to reflect tribal values and their way of life, and they feel they ought to influence and exercise control over this education."

... And Justice for All, The NEA Executive Committee Study Group Reports on Ethnic Minority Concerns (Washington, D.C.: National Education Association, June 1987).

Asian and Pacific Islander

The Asian and Pacific Islander population is comprised of many different ethnicities and languages. Asian and Pacific Islanders hail from a multitude of cultures and political, religious, and economic backgrounds. The differences among Asian and Pacific Islander groups are exacerbated by the length of time each group has been exposed to Western ways. Differences are widespread between new groups of Asian immigrants—such as the Hmong refugees from the Laotian mountains—and Pacific Islanders from American and trust territories, between native Hawaiians and longtime Americans of Japanese descent. And differences also exist between generations within the same ethnic groups.

In the U.S. context, the different Asian and Pacific Islander groups operate in a common political milieu. All individuals from these groups—no matter how different their cultural groups may be from each other—are identified as Asian or Pacific Islander. Employers tend to perceive Asians and Pacific Islanders as a source of cheap, passive, one-dimensional labor. Many Americans in mainstream society perceive Asians and Pacific Islanders as outsiders who are taking away the benefits that are due "real" Americans. These attitudes tend to make Asians and Pacific Islanders easy targets for hostility in the workplace, in public housing, in small business, and in college admissions. Trade deficits between the U.S. and Asia that affect jobs and job opportunities in America are still another obstacle that makes life difficult for Asians and Pacific Islanders.

Black

The more than 30 years that have elapsed since the 1954 *Brown* decision have witnessed major initiatives aimed at bettering the status—particularly the educational status—of Black Americans. But despite these events and historic developments—despite countless marches and protests, despite the passage of federal civil rights laws and comprehensive federal education legislation, despite the Kerner Commission Report of 1967, despite continued approval by the Black community of increased taxes to support public schools, despite frequent reports on the status of education for Blacks in the United States, and despite improved access for many Black students to quality K-12 education and college admission—Black parents, Black students, the Black community, and the education community in general are today confronted with tremendous educational challenges for Black students—the most serious since 1954.

Among these challenges: a high dropout and teen pregnancy rate among Black youth, financially poor and segregated schools, a lack of early intervention programs, limited support systems and positive role models for Blacks in general and Black males specifically, a shortage of both college scholarships and Black teachers, inappropriate testing, racial discrimination, and relentless poverty.

Hispanic

Hispanics are the nation's fastest growing ethnic group. Their growth rate is five times that of the general population. In 1985, the U.S. Census Bureau reported 16.9 million Hispanics, an increase of 16 percent since the 1980 Census. Hispanics comprise 7.2 percent of the country's total population.

Mexican Americans, who doubled their population in the decade between 1970 and 1980, are the largest subgroup, comprising over 60 percent of all Hispanics with a population of 10 million. They are followed by Puerto Ricans with 2 million; Cubans with 1 million; and a Central, South American, and other Spanish origin group of 3 million.

Hispanics are both natives of and immigrants to this nation. Hispanic American culture today reflects both the heritage of the Native American Indians who inhabited what are now the states of the Southwest and the heritage of Spanish settlers to the New World. The first European settlers within what we now know as the continental United States were Spanish. Indeed, the Spanish-speaking communities of Santa Fe, New Mexico, and St. Augustine, Florida, predate the landing of the Pilgrims at Plymouth Rock.

B. WHO WILL TEACH MINORITY YOUTH?
by Wali Gill

The decline in the number of minority teachers in this country is of grave concern to all persons truly interested in today's youth. Minority teachers play a critical role as empathetic mentors for minority students and as nonstereotypical examples for majority students.

In the U.S. today, the student populations of many urban—and some suburban—districts are becoming "minority majority." Non-white children constitute about one-third of the preschool population, and their number is growing more rapidly than that of white children.[1] By the year 2000, African-American and Hispanic students together are expected to make up one-third of public school enrollments.[2] The following data, estimates from the National Center for Educational Statistics for 1984-85 (the last year for which data are available), show, for whites, African-Americans, Hispanics, Asian-Americans, and Native Americans, percentages of students in public schools and percentages of teachers from these groups teaching in public schools.[3]

	Students	Teachers
White	71.2%	89.6%
African-American	16.2%	6.9%
Hispanic	9.1%	1.9%
Asian-American	2.5%	0.9%
Native American	0.9%	0.6%

This trend is also evident at the college level. Although there is an increasing number of minorities in the general population—an estimated 21 percent—they make up only 17 percent of the enrollment in higher education.[4] Of those enrolled in colleges and universities, few intend to enter teaching, now that other and higher-paying careers are open to them; and the data on education majors document this. During the 1980-81 school year, 17 percent of education degrees went to African-Americans and His-

---

Educational Leadership, May 1989, p. 83. Copyright © 1989 Association for Supervision and Curriculum Development. All rights reserved. Used with permission of the Association for Supervision and Curriculum Development.

panics, while during 1984–85 only 10.4 percent of education degrees were conferred on African-Americans, Hispanics, Asians, and Native Americans combined.[5] Teacher education institutions are renewing their efforts to recruit and retain minority students.[6,7]

Regardless of minority teacher-student ratios, the "humanistic" and primary responsibility of educating ethnic youth remains with minority group members, who continue to turn toward each other for strength, support, and direction. In the past, African-American colleges, although representing only 5 percent of U.S. universities and colleges in total enrollment, have produced 66 percent of African-American teachers.[8] Further, national and community ethnic-group organizations must continue to provide after-school educational and cultural opportunities and forge partnerships with local businesses, government, and churches.

The real teachers, however, are the parents of ethnic-group children. These parents are the mainstays for their children's personal growth and school achievement. Parents must communicate interpersonal skills, enforce domestic responsibilities with both daughters and sons, establish high goals, and encourage their children to dream. Through demonstrated behaviors, teachers must reinforce present-day parental efforts with the old-fashioned remedies, such as "You have to work twice as hard as others . . . be a credit to your race . . . and don't let me hear anything bad about you." Both minority teachers and parents live their lives under varying degrees of racism, prejudice, discrimination, and social contradictions; nevertheless, both are leading forces for their students and children, instructing by whatever behavior they demonstrate. Where are the minority teachers? They are in the homes of ethnic-group children. They just have to speak up.

NOTES

1. H. L. Hodgkinson, telephone interview, October 18, 1988; and "Here They Come, Ready or Not," *Education Week* (May 1986).
2. H. L. Hodgkinson, "The Right Schools for the Right Kids," *Educational Leadership* 45, no. 5 (February 1988): 10-14.
3. National Center for Educational Statistics, *Estimate of School Statistics* (Washington, D.C.: U.S. Government Printing Office, 1988).
4. American Council of Education, *Fifth Annual Status Report on Minorities in Higher Education* (Washington, D.C.: American Council of Education, 1986).
5. W. Trent, "Equity Considerations in Higher Education: Race and Sex Differences in Degree, Attainment, and Major Field from 1976 through 1981," *American Journal of Education* 92, no. 3 (May 1986): 280-305.
6. E. J. Middleton; E. J. Mason; W. E. Stilwell; and W. C. Parker, "A Model for Recruitment and Retention of Minority Students in Teacher Education Programs," *Journal of Teacher Education* 14, no. 18 (January-February 1988).
7. A. M. Garibaldi, "Recruitment, Admissions, and Standards: Black Teachers and the Holmes and Carnegie Reports," *Metropolitan Education* 13, no. 3 (Summer 1987): 17-23.
8. V. L. Clark, "Teacher Education at Historically Black Institutions in the Aftermath of the Holmes/Carnegie Reports," *Planning and Changing* 18, no. 2 (Summer 1987): 74-79.

THE CONTRIBUTORS

Livingston Alexander is Department Head and Professor, School of Education, Georgia Southern College, Statesboro.

Denise Alston is Senior Education Associate, Children's Defense Fund, Washington, D.C.

Bennett F. Berhow is Associate Dean, College of Education, University of Wisconsin-Whitewater.

Mary Gendernalik Cooper is Executive Director, Teacher Education Reform Projects, San Diego State University, California.

Jody Daughtry is Associate Professor, Teacher Education Department, California State University, Fresno.

Mary E. Dilworth is Director of Research and Information Services, American Association of Colleges for Teacher Education, and Director of the ERIC Clearinghouse on Teacher Education, Washington, D.C.

Antoine M. Garibaldi is Chairman/Associate Professor of Education at Xavier University, New Orleans.

Ann Richardson Gayles is Professor of Education, College of Education, Florida Agricultural and Mechanical University, Tallahassee.

Bruce G. Gordon is Associate Professor and Recruitment Facilitator for the School of Education, Auburn University, Montgomery, Alabama.

Nathaniel Jackson is Program Officer at the Southern Education Foundation, Atlanta, Georgia.

Wanda M. Johnson is Assistant Professor, Department of Psychology and Personnel Services, and Coordinator of the Guidance and Counseling Programs for School Counselors, Central State University, Edmond, Oklahoma.

Debra Knowles was formerly Director, Minority Teacher Preparation Program, University of Wisconsin-Whitewater.

Evangie H. McGlon is Associate Professor, Department of Applied Behavioral Studies in Education, Oklahoma State University, Stillwater.

John W. Miller is Dean, School of Education, Georgia Southern College, Statesboro.

Ann I. Morey is Dean, College of Education, San Diego State University, California.

Gay C. Neuberger is a Research Associate in the Office of the Dean of Education, Oklahoma State University, Stillwater.

Harvey Pressman is President, Corporation for Opportunity Expansion, Inc., Newton, Massachusetts.

Julia L. Willard is Associate Professor of Education, Director of Laboratory Programs, and Recruitment Coordinator for the School of Education, Auburn University, Montgomery, Alabama.

Elaine P. Witty is Dean, School of Education, Norfolk State University, Virginia.